JOSEPH
'GOD Planned It for Good'

by Theodore H. Epp

Director
Back to the Bible Broadcast

A
BACK TO THE BIBLE
PUBLICATION

Back to the Bible
Lincoln, Nebraska 68501

133,000 printed to date—1979
(5-8750—3M—119)
ISBN 0-8474-1283-0

Printed in the United States of America

Foreword

It is a timeless principle that "all things work together for good to them that love God, to them who are the called according to his purpose" (Rom. 8:28). Joseph's life was an Old Testament demonstration of Romans 8:28.

Even though all things work together for good for the believer, it is not always evident what God is trying to accomplish in his life. Never has this been more true than in the case of Joseph. In fact, God kept His overall plan from Joseph so that He could teach him needed lessons. God wanted Joseph to have explicit faith in Him in any kind of circumstance. The process which God used was a series of tests in the different areas of Joseph's life. There were the tests of adversity, body, soul, prosperity, and inner man. These tests were applied to Joseph in his experiences in the pit, Potiphar's house, and the prison, and prepared him to be the prime minister of Egypt.

Joseph's life demonstrates how God chooses and molds a man in order to use him to accomplish His overall purpose. It was in God's program to have Jacob's family go to Egypt in order to become a great nation and later return to the land of Canaan. But to accomplish this, God had to send His servant ahead to prepare the way.

Joseph's confidence was not in his ability to understand his circumstances; his confidence was in the God of all circumstances.

As you study Joseph's life you will be encouraged to trust God in every situation. Your heart will be touched as you see how tender and forgiving Joseph was to his brothers after all they had done to him. From Joseph's life you will gain confidence that God is working out His will through you even though you may not realize it. As with Joseph, any present suffering you are going through may be God's way of preparing you for a significant future task. God's ultimate purpose in working everything together for our good is that we might "be conformed to the image of his Son" (Rom. 8:29). When you grasp the reality of the sovereignty of God in your daily circumstances, you will be able to say as did Joseph, "God planned it for good. . . ." (Gen. 50:20, Berkeley).

—Harold J. Berry
Instructor
Grace College of the Bible
Omaha, Nebraska

Contents

Chapter 1

'A Man in Whom the Spirit of God Is'

Even the God-rejecting world of Joseph's day testified that Joseph was a man of God. After Joseph had been brought from prison and had interpreted Pharaoh's dream, "Pharaoh said unto his servants, Can we find such a one as this is, a man in whom the Spirit of God is?" (Gen. 41:38). This phrase fittingly described Joseph, and it was because the Spirit of God was in him that he was able to say after his gross mistreatment by his brothers, "God planned it for good" (50:20, Berkeley).

In the Book of Genesis there are seven significant men mentioned after the time of Adam, and each of them represents various aspects of faith.

Abel, who offered a more excellent sacrifice, represents redemption through faith. Enoch, who was taken to heaven without dying, represents the walk of faith for he "walked with God" (5:22). Noah, who built the ark and sought to persuade others to enter, represents the confession of faith. Abraham, who trusted God in the face of insurmountable obstacles, represents the obedience of faith. Isaac, who submitted to his earthly father and unresistingly yielded to his Heavenly Father, represents the patience of faith. Jacob, who experienced extreme heights and depths in his life, represents the training of faith.

In the life of Joseph there is a twofold emphasis—the testing and the triumph of faith. In his life we see in action the principle stated in I Peter 1:7: "That the trial of your faith, being much more precious than of gold that perisheth, though it be tried with fire, might be found unto praise and honour and glory at the appearing of Jesus Christ." Joseph's life of faith represents both the testing and the triumph.

In another comparison of some of these men's lives, it can be said that Abraham illustrates the doctrine of election. God chose him to be the progenitor of a nation that was later known as the Israelites. It is God's prerogative to choose whom He pleases. He does not choose some to be saved and some to be lost, but rather He desires that all should be saved and come to repentance (II Pet. 3:9). However, when it has to do with kind and place of service, God definitely chooses some to serve him in distinct ways.

Isaac's life illustrates the doctrine of sonship. The first son born to Abraham was Ishmael, but he was born after the flesh and was rejected by God as the one in whom His promises would be fulfilled. God refuses to use that which is born after the flesh, regardless of how good it is. On the other hand, Isaac was born by a miracle of God and was given the full position and the rights of sonship.

The life of Jacob illustrates the conflict between the two natures in the believer. In his life there was the battle spoken of in Galatians 5:16,17: "This I say then, Walk in the Spirit, and ye shall not fulfil the lust of the flesh. For the flesh lusteth against the Spirit, and the Spirit against the flesh: and these are contrary the one to the other: so that ye cannot do the things that ye would." It took the discipline of God to cause Jacob to want to yield to his new nature instead of to his old nature.

Joseph's life illustrates our divine heirship—that we are heirs of God. The Bible teaches clearly what the prerequisites of heirship are. In particular, spiritual heirship is preceded by suffering. Suffering always precedes glory. The Christian suffers beforehand so he might be a partaker of the glory to follow. The Apostle Paul wrote: "The Spirit itself beareth witness with our spirit, that we are the children of God: and if children, then heirs; heirs of God, and joint-heirs with Christ; if so be that we suffer with him, that we may be also glorified together" (Rom. 8:16,17).

As we consider the life of Joseph, it is apparent to us that he had an almost flawless character. There are two men in the Bible about whom nothing negative is recorded. These men are Joseph and Daniel. This does not mean that the men were without sin, but it was not God's purpose in recording their lives to emphasize that which was negative.

In Joseph, God wanted to show us how a person can live honorably before God regardless of his heredity and environment. In the midst of the corruption of his day, Joseph lived a godly life. Even while he was in prison on false charges, Joseph's life was so glorifying to God that he gained favor in the eyes of the jailor, and the jailor placed Joseph in charge of all the prisoners (Gen. 39:21-23). No wonder it was later obvious to Pharaoh that Joseph was "a man in whom the Spirit of God is" (41:38). Only a person who had as close a walk with God as Joseph had would have been able at a later time to victoriously say, "God planned it for good" (50:20, Berkeley).

The secret of Joseph's life was the indwelling Spirit. But he had nothing that present-day believers do not have. Concerning all believers it can be said, "Christ in you, the hope of glory" (Col. 1:27). Christ is in us to produce a righteous character. Sometimes it is necessary that this be done through suffering. Although it is burdensome at the time, suffering is used by God to mold the Christian into what He wants him to be.

It was because of the Apostle Paul's realization that Christ was in him that he was able to say, "I can do all things through Christ which strengtheneth me" (Phil. 4:13). Also, because of this truth, he was able to write: "And [so that you can know and understand] what is the immeasurable and unlimited and surpassing greatness of His power in and for us who believe, as demonstrated in the working of His mighty strength" (Eph. 1:19, Amp.). And, assuming Paul to have been the writer of Hebrews, he was also able to say, "Strengthen (complete, perfect) and make you what you ought to be, and equip you with everything good that you may carry out His will; [while He Himself] works in you and accomplishes that which is pleasing in His sight, through Jesus Christ, the Messiah; to Whom be the glory forever and ever—to the ages of the ages. Amen—so be it" (Heb. 13:21, Amp.). From these verses it is apparent that we believers living in the 20th century have the same privilege that Joseph had. Therefore, might our study of his life challenge and encourage us to say, "If Joseph could live such a flawless, or victorious, life under those extreme circumstances, then certainly it is possible for me to live a victorious life today."

The things which Joseph suffered caused him to learn obedience. Even of Christ we are told, "Though he were a Son, yet learned he obedience by the things which he suffered" (Heb. 5:8). Certainly this was never more true than in His experience of the cross. Paul said of Christ, "And being found in fashion as a man, he humbled himself, and became obedient unto death, even the death of the cross" (Phil. 2:8).

We are helped in our understanding of Joseph's life if we realize that he had to learn obedience the hard way. We, too, often have to learn it the hard way. But those who desire to be spiritually mature must realize that there is no shortcut to spirituality. How thankful we can be that we have Christ living within us to make us into what He wants us to be—this is our hope of glory.

Chapter 2

Joseph's Early Life

Very little is known about the first 17 years of Joseph's life. We do know, however, that he was the firstborn of Rachel while Jacob was serving Laban at Haran. At Joseph's birth, Rachel "called his name Joseph; and said, The Lord shall add to me another son" (Gen. 30:24). After Joseph was born, Jacob said to Laban, "Send me away, that I may go unto mine own place, and to my country" (30:25).

Joseph was possibly five or six years old when they left Haran. Certainly, he was affected both by heredity and environment. He would have witnessed, for instance, Jacob's flight after he had stolen away from Laban. Joseph would have witnessed Laban's pursuit of his father, Jacob, and his furious anger at Jacob's having taken his family and livestock and having sneaked away.

Joseph would have witnessed the coming of his uncle, Esau, with 400 men to meet Jacob. Joseph would have well remembered the fear that filled the whole camp of his father Jacob. At such a young age, these things would have made deep impressions on him. But, no doubt, he also witnessed the return of his father after his all-night encounter at Peniel. Joseph would have noticed the change in his father as he returned limping and with brokenness of heart before God. This, too, would have made a deep impression upon him.

Joseph would have known about his sister being defiled. He would have known the resulting frightening experience at Shechem when two of his older brothers committed the terrible sin of killing many people. He would also have

11

known about how his father finally came back to Bethel. Joseph would have seen the altar there, and this would have made a great impression in his early life.

Then there was the death of his mother when he was very young. He would always remember how heartbroken his father was because Rachel had been so precious to him. I can imagine how Joseph felt. I was only six when my mother died, so I can understand something of what Joseph went through.

As time passed, Joseph would see the bitterness and jealousies which resulted from his father's having four wives. Joseph would feel the bickering and bitterness among the women and children. Joseph's early life was by no means a sheltered one. However, his life is one of the most fascinating lives in all history. It has all the elements for a great story — ambition, youth, beauty, temptation, suffering, sorrow, jealousy, hate, forgiveness.

Joseph's adult life would be greatly influenced by what he experienced in his early life. Modern psychology tells us that children are deeply affected by both their heredity and environment. Although there were many negative things about Joseph's early years, there are also indications of some good training during this formative time of his life.

Although Joseph's mother, Rachel, died when he was at a very tender age, she must have had a tremendous influence on his life. Joseph's desire to obey God later in life was most probably directly connected to his mother's godly influence on him as a young child.

In this way, Joseph was like Moses, whose impressions of early youth also bore great fruit. Moses never forgot his training. No doubt it significantly contributed to his finally joining himself to the people of Israel. The divine commentary of his life is: "By faith Moses, when he was come to years, refused to be called the son of Pharaoh's daughter; choosing rather to suffer affliction with the people of God, than to enjoy the pleasures of sin for a season" (Heb. 11:24,25).

Joseph was younger and was probably even closer to Jacob, because of Rachel, than the rest of the sons. Therefore it is likely that Jacob spent more time with him and told him about many of these things and how his own heart had been affected.

This emphasizes that we are responsible to train our children at an early age. The main reason we have a generation of young people who act as they do today is that they did not receive the proper training when they were very young. Too often, when there are small children in the home, the father is on one shift, the mother is on another shift, and the children are left to shift for themselves. Frequently it is a baby-sitter who has the responsibility of rearing the children. I realize there are some cases where this is necessary. My concern, however, is for those situations where it is not necessary but where it is done because the parents have their hearts set on material things. The mother belongs in the home to train the children in their formative years.

As we consider Joseph's life, we find him to be a young man who became a slave at the age of 17 and who rose to be the premier of the most powerful nation of his day by the time he was 30. His early training in the home prepared him for what he suffered in the process. Because of his home training, he had faith to trust God in spite of the circumstances. No doubt it was largely his early training that helped him to remain morally pure in his youth and to take a lonely stand against sin—even in the family circle.

Joseph at 17

After the record of Joseph's birth in Genesis 30:23,24, very little is said of him until he was 17 years of age. Genesis 37 begins the detailed record of his life. The first two verses of this chapter tell us: "And Jacob dwelt in the land wherein his father was a stranger, in the land of Canaan. These are the generations of Jacob. Joseph, being seventeen years old, was feeding the flock with his brethren; and the lad was with the sons of Bilhah, and with the sons of Zilpah, his father's wives: and Joseph brought unto his father their evil report."

In addition to the children of Bilhah and Zilpah, the children of Leah were also Joseph's early companions. The half brothers of Joseph were unfit companions for spiritual encouragement. They had naturally been affected by the life they had witnessed in Haran and the conflict they had seen between their father, Jacob, and Laban. They were also affected by the jealousies they saw in their homes among their mothers. These children were older than Joseph and had received their early impressions from the old Jacob—the Jacob before Peniel. These impressions came before their father was mellowed in spiritual things. Perhaps you say, "Yes, but couldn't they have learned differently after Jacob became Israel and had his experience with God and began to really walk with God?" This might seem logical, but indelible impressions had already been made on their lives.

Perhaps you came to know the Lord in your adult life and are now concerned about the way your children are going. During their formative years you were not a Christian, and now that they are older they continue to go the way of their early training. Some say that a child learns the greatest percentage of his basic attitudes before he is three years of age. In a special way, it is what is done in these formative years that determines the direction of his life when he is older.

Perhaps you were a Christian during your children's impressionable years, but you were spiritually negligent or did not know the importance of reading the Bible to them, having them memorize Scripture, and singing songs which fixed their hearts on God. We reap what we sow. If we have not trained our children in the way they should go, we cannot expect that they will walk in it when they are older.

Regrettably, we cannot go back and change the past, but this shows us the importance of training children in their formative years. Those who know Christ as Saviour and have children in this stage of life should be sure that they are doing their best for the Lord and that they are not sacrificing the training of the children for extra money that mother may be able to earn.

Joseph's older brothers were a bad influence on the younger ones and Joseph brought to his father "their evil report" (v. 2). Joseph's sense of family duty compelled him to report honestly to his father the evil conduct of his older brothers. Some would take from this incident that Joseph's heart was not right and, as children would say, he was being a "tattletale." Talebearing, as such, is despicable—but there is a time to speak. There is a time when silence can actually be criminal. In Joseph's case there seems to have been no exaggerations, no malice, and no personal ends to be served; thus, no one could really blame Joseph. From every indication, Joseph told his father these things because of Joseph's deep convictions of right and wrong. He felt his father ought to know what his own sons were doing.

The Scriptures comment, "Now Israel [Jacob] loved Joseph more than all his children, because he was the son of his old age: and he made him a coat of many colours. And when his brethren saw that their father loved him more than all his brethren, they hated him, and could not speak peaceably unto him" (vv. 3,4). Joseph's telling on his brothers only made their hatred for him more intense. But it is important to know why they hated him. The Scriptures say that Jacob "made him a coat of many colours" (v. 3). The Amplified Bible makes this even more clear when it says that Jacob "made him a [distinctive] long tunic with sleeves." The important thing about the coat was not its colors but the fact that it was a special coat because of its significant meaning.

The background to this is found in I Chronicles 5:1,2: "Now the sons of Reuben the firstborn of Israel, (for he was the firstborn; but, forasmuch as he defiled his father's bed, his birthright was given unto the sons of Joseph the son of Israel, and the genealogy is not to be reckoned after the birthright. For Judah prevailed above his brethren, and of him came the chief ruler; but the birthright was Joseph's)." Reuben had committed fornication with his father's concubine; therefore, the birthright was transferred from Reuben to Joseph. Reuben was the firstborn of Leah, and Joseph was the firstborn of Rachel. Because of Reuben's sin, the birthright was transferred from the firstborn of one to the firstborn of the other.

The coat that Jacob made for Joseph designated that Joseph was to be the heir to the birthright. His brothers knew this and it was the main reason they hated him and could not talk peaceably with him. Add to all this Joseph's purity of life and moral growth—and the irritation was unbearable.

Joseph's Dreams

Then "Joseph dreamed a dream, and he told it his brethren: and they hated him yet the more" (Gen. 37:5). Their hatred was at the exploding point—they could stand Joseph no longer. Knowing from his brothers' acts at Shechem what atrocities they were capable of, certainly Joseph had reason to fear for his life.

The situation was not helped by Joseph's giving his brothers a detailed account of his dream. "He said unto them, Hear, I pray you, this dream which I have dreamed: for, behold, we were binding sheaves in the field, and, lo, my sheaf arose, and also stood upright; and, behold, your sheaves stood round about, and made obeisance to my sheaf. And his brethren said to him, Shalt thou indeed reign over us? or shalt thou indeed have dominion over us? And they hated him yet the more for his dreams, and for his words" (v. 6-8).

Then Joseph had another dream and told his brothers about it. He said, "Behold, I have dreamed a dream more; and, behold, the sun and the moon and the eleven stars made obeisance to me" (v. 9). This dream served only to underscore the truth of the first dream. The brothers understood clearly what was implied and they were furious in their hatred of Joseph.

When Joseph told the second dream to his father and his brothers, "his father rebuked him, and said unto him, What is this dream that thou hast dreamed? Shall I and thy mother and thy brethren indeed come to bow down ourselves to thee to the earth?" (v. 10).

The Scriptures record that there was a twofold response to Joseph's dreams: His brothers "envied him; but his father observed the saying" (Gen. 37:11). His brothers were jealous of him, but his father pondered and heeded what Joseph said. He began to reflect on how all this might fit into God's program, although at first he had rebuked Joseph.

These prophetic dreams were God-given, and we are not told what Joseph's attitude was as he told his father and brothers about them. Whether it was wise or unwise for Joseph to have told them, God permitted him to do so and even used the brothers' reaction as a means toward fulfilling the prophetic aspect revealed in the dreams.

Commenting on these incidents, the New Testament says, "And the patriarchs, moved with envy, sold Joseph into Egypt: but God was with him" (Acts 7:9). So it was with Jesus. Pilate knew that the people wanted Jesus crucified because of the envy of their hearts. They could no longer take what He was saying. Although He was rejected of men, God was with Him.

When Jacob learned of Joseph's dreams, he pondered the matter in his heart. This reminds us of the New Testament incident where Jesus was in the temple at the age of 12, astonishing those present with his understanding and answers. At first his parents were not able to find Him, but when at last they did, Jesus said to them, "How is it that ye sought me? Wist ye not that I must be about my Father's business?" (Luke 2:49). He went with them to Nazareth and was subject unto them "but his mother kept all these sayings in her heart" (v. 51). No doubt Mary pondered not only what Jesus said in the temple but also what the angels, shepherds and others had said of Him at His birth.

Many times in the years to follow, Joseph must have wondered about his dreams and their fulfillment. The next 13 years of his life were filled with many tests and trials. Humanly speaking, they all seemed to stem from the time when he incited his brothers' hatred by sharing his dreams with them.

Had Joseph been looking at only the circumstances, he would have despaired of all hope, but his trust was in God. God's ways are mysterious; they are beyond man's comprehension. As God sovereignly works, man is often unable to understand why he is being led down a certain path. Proverbs 20:24 says, "Man's goings are of the Lord; how can a man then understand his own way?" Believers need confidence in God that He will accomplish His will whether they understand it at the time or not. Speaking of the confidence that believers can have, the Apostle Paul said, "We know that all things work together for good to them that love God, to them who are the called according to his purpose. For whom he did foreknow, he also did predestinate to be conformed to the image of his Son, that he might be the firstborn among many brethren" (Rom. 8:28,29). Even when the circumstances look hopeless, the believer can have confidence that God knows what He is doing and that He is working out His perfect will through the believer's life.

God Uses Processes

During the next 13 years of Joseph's life, he must often have asked himself, How are these circumstances working for the glory of God? He must have recognized that he was a chosen vessel of God, even though how God was going to use him in fulfilling His will was a complete mystery. In this sense, he was no doubt like Moses of whom it is said in Acts 7:25, "For he supposed his brethren would have understood how that God by his hand would deliver them: but they understood not." Frequently people do not understand when God is leading one of His servants in a special way. Their reaction is often the same as Joseph's brothers—envy. Joseph desired to please God, but far from his mind were any thoughts of captivity in a foreign country and all that he might have to endure there. But God not only had a far-reaching program but also a process in His divine plan.

God had chosen Abraham to become the father of a great nation. Abraham's grandson, Jacob, had 12 sons who were to be the foundation of the coming kingdom. In Canaan, however, the nation's existence was threatened. The Canaanites might either annihilate this small band of people for intruding on their territory, or the Israelites might become amalgamated with the Canaanites and lose their distinction as a people. In His wisdom, God used a process so that the Israelites would remain a unique people and survive to become a great nation. Jacob's sons showed very little concern for separation, so God's plan was to move Jacob and his family to Egypt. Later, when Jacob was considering going down to Egypt, God said to him, "I am God, the God of thy father: fear not to go down into Egypt; for I will there make of thee a great nation: I will go down with thee into Egypt; and I will also surely bring thee up again" (Gen. 46:3,4). God had to use a process to accomplish His will for the nation.

We, too, need to submit ourselves wholly to God so that He can work His will through us. Frequently, we may not be able to understand what God is working to accomplish in our lives, but in such times we need to think of portions such as Psalm 37. Here we are told, "Commit thy way unto the Lord; trust also in him; and he shall bring it to pass" (v. 5). When we commit our way to the Lord, the result is that "he [God] shall bring forth thy righteousness as the light, and thy judgment as the noonday" (v. 6). So the admonition is: "Rest in the Lord, and wait patiently for him: fret not thyself because of him who prospereth in his way, because of the man who bringeth wicked devices to pass. Cease from anger, and forsake wrath: fret not thyself in any wise to do evil. For evildoers shall be cut off: but those that wait upon the Lord, they shall inherit the earth. For yet a little while, and the wicked shall not be: yea, thou shalt diligently consider his place, and it shall not be. But the meek shall inherit the earth; and shall delight themselves in the abundance of peace" (vv. 7-11). The rest of Psalm 37 also tells us what our attitudes should be when our way is uncertain or when we cannot understand what God is doing in our lives.

Sent on a Mission

After Joseph's encounter with his brothers about his dreams, they "went to feed their father's flock in Shechem" (Gen. 37:12). We are not sure how much time had elapsed since the incidents of the dreams. But verse 13 continues the account by saying, "And Israel [Jacob] said unto Joseph, Do not thy brethren feed the flock in Shechem? come, and I will send thee unto them. And he said to him, Here am I."

It was earlier at Shechem that Jacob's sons, Simeon and Levi, had killed many people because of the sin committed against their sister, Dinah. At that time, Jacob had said to Simeon and Levi, "Ye have troubled me to make me to stink among the inhabitants of the land, among the Canaanites and the Perizzites: and I being few in number, they shall gather themselves together against me, and slay me; and I shall be destroyed, I and my house" (34:30).

So Joseph was sent to his brothers, who were now where these atrocities had been committed. Jacob was probably concerned about the physical well-being of his sons, since there still might be reprisals because of the previous incident. In spite of Joseph's troubles with his brothers, he said, "Here am I." Joseph put himself at the disposal of God through obedience to his father. This basic attitude of obedience was certainly one of the significant reasons that Joseph was so greatly used of God in the years that followed.

Jacob gave Joseph further instructions concerning all that he was to investigate. Jacob said, "Go, I pray thee, see whether it be well with thy brethren, and well with the flocks; and bring me word again. So he sent him out of the vale of Hebron, and he came to Shechem" (37:14).

Joseph was not able to find his brothers. A man found him wandering in the field and told him, "They are departed hence; for I heard them say, Let us go to Dothan" (v. 17).

Joseph then went in search of his brothers at Dothan. They saw him coming while he was still far away. The Scriptures say, "And when they saw him afar off, even before he came near unto them, they conspired against him to slay him. And they said one to another, Behold, this dreamer cometh" (vv. 18,19). These words reveal the bad attitude of Joseph's brothers, and Joseph was about to meet the first of many serious tests in his life.

The Test of Adversity

Joseph's brothers plotted and said, "Come now therefore, and let us slay him, and cast him into some pit, and we will say, Some evil beast hath devoured him: and we shall see what will become of his dreams" (v. 20).

In Joseph's tests we see that trials and temptations involve both God and Satan. So it is in our lives. Satan's objective is to bring about our ruin; God's objective is to establish us in holiness.

In I Peter 5:8 we are warned: "Be sober, be vigilant; because your adversary the devil, as a roaring lion, walketh about, seeking whom he may devour." However, verse 10 in this same passage tells us, "But the God of all grace, who hath called us unto his eternal glory by Christ Jesus, after that ye have suffered a while, make you perfect, stablish, strengthen, settle you." These two verses give us the objectives of Satan and of God in our testing. God uses trials for our benefit. Hebrews 12:11 tells us, "Now no chastening for the present seemeth to be joyous, but grievous: nevertheless afterward it yieldeth the peaceable fruit of righteousness unto them which are exercised thereby."

God allows tests to separate the gold from the dross. Satan probes us with the intent of finding our weak spots, for his objective is always evil. Both of these aspects are seen in Joseph's testings. God was seeking to prepare him for a very special task, whereas Satan was trying to spoil God's purpose for Joseph's life.

The brothers first planned to murder Joseph and then to deceive their father into believing some beast had devoured him. What was really bothering the brothers was obvious in their statement: "And we shall see what will become of his dreams" (Gen. 37:20). Joseph was a righteous young man; he walked before God. But such a life as his exposed the sins of his brothers, so they plotted to do away with him.

The same was true in the time of Christ's earthly life. The religious leaders of His day hated Him and were jealous of Him because His righteous life exposed their unrighteousness. The principle is still true today. A godly life exposes the sins of others and causes them to want to take action to keep the godly person out of their way.

Joseph had especially antagonized his brothers in the past because he was anxious for righteousness and had reported their wicked ways to his father. Joseph was a prophet for truth even in his teens. We need more Josephs today—those who are able to stand against the fickleness of their generation. But unless we give more attention to the proper training of our children and young people, we are not going to produce any Josephs.

When Joseph's brothers plotted against him, "Reuben heard it, and he delivered him out of their hands; and said, Let us not kill him. And Reuben said unto them, Shed no blood, but cast him into this pit that is in the wilderness, and lay no hand upon him; that he might rid him out of their hands, to deliver him to his father again. And it came to pass, when Joseph was come unto his brethren, that they stript Joseph out of his coat, his coat of many colours that was on him; and they took him, and cast him into a pit: and the pit was empty, there was no water in it" (vv. 21-24).

Although Reuben was not known for his stability, he came up with a plan whereby he thought he could deliver Joseph safely back to his father. Reuben's suggestion was used of God, for it was in His plan to preserve Joseph and have him sent to Egypt so he would be there to preserve the nation later. Although Satan was seeking to destroy God's plan, God overruled so that even unstable Reuben was used to make a suggestion that fit into God's program. However, from the human standpoint, Reuben's plan failed because he was not able to return Joseph to his father.

They stripped Joseph of his garment of many colors—the garment that was so special because it designated the rights of the firstborn. Joseph was not only to have the birthright, but God had shown him through dreams that he was also to have a royal position.

Joseph's brothers were not able to stand the sight of him nor of his coat because of what it represented. Having cast him into a pit, they "sat down to eat bread" (v. 25). They celebrated their apparent victory over Joseph.

A Place of Death

We do not know how many hopeless and hungry hours Joseph spent in the pit—possibly it was for an entire night. Although Reuben intended to deliver Joseph back to his father, no doubt the intent of the rest of the brothers was to let Joseph starve in the pit. They had cast him into a place of death.

Even in this there is a spiritual lesson for us. Resurrection comes only out of death. We must recognize ourselves as dead with Christ before we can experience the victorious life. Galatians 2:20 says, "I am [literally, "I have been"] crucified with Christ: nevertheless I live; yet not I, but Christ liveth in me: and the life which I now live in the flesh I live by the faith of the Son of God, who loved me, and gave himself for me." The believer has gone through death with Christ and also through the resurrection with Christ. The believer has Christ within him and he is to live his life by the faith of the Son of God. All of these benefits must be appropriated by faith.

Joseph's night alone with God in the pit was really what he needed. Although Joseph lived a righteous life, he was not yet ready for what God purposed to do with him. So God brought him to this place of death to prepare him to live. We, too, must pass through the place of death to self before we become useful to God.

Joseph's being alone in the pit where God could deal with him is a reminder of the way God worked with Jacob. God dealt with Jacob when he was alone at Bethel and then some 20 years later when he was alone at Peniel. Both of these were significant times in the progress of Jacob's life. Frequently, God is able to best deal with us when we are alone. Even Christ spent agonizing hours alone in Gethsemane before He was betrayed and finally crucified.

For Joseph, the night in the pit was not a night of defeat but a night of victory. If there were any self-ambition and dreams of self-importance left in Joseph, the night in the pit in hopeless despair would have removed them. Therefore, Joseph's experience in the pit was the beginning of a victorious life. He was now completely under God's control, for any selfish desires had been reckoned dead. Joseph realized that his dreams were God's revelation to him and, therefore, it was God's responsibility to fulfill the dreams. Joseph was not to try to fulfill the dreams on his own, but he was to make himself available to God so that God could fulfill the dreams through him. Because he was only 17 years of age when the dreams came to him, perhaps there was some youthful pride in them. If so, the experience of the pit would have completely removed it.

Reuben's Compromise

Reuben's motives to deliver Joseph were good, but his character was weak. He sought to change circumstances but failed to protest outright and to call sin "sin." He thought if he could change the circumstances he would be able to do something for Joseph, but there is no indication that he rebuked his brothers for what they were plotting. He feared to face the facts of sin. No doubt he feared his brothers more than he feared God. Reuben was not courageous enough to say to his brothers, "This is sin and we don't dare do it." Because he did not squarely face the issue of sin, later he was guilty of going along with his brothers in deceiving their father.

Sin that is not faced outright will always conquer in the end. There are those who believe one should join questionable organizations with the hope of somehow reaching people in those organizations and pointing them in the right direction. However, it is impossible to win the world by becoming like the world. We cannot conquer self by self and we cannot conquer the world by the world. We need to have an outreach so that we can win others to Christ, but we should never become a partaker in their sins. Christ identified Himself with humanity, but He never took part in man's sin in order to get a hearing for the gospel.

Regardless of the approach used to reach others for Christ, there should never be compromise with the world or the bringing of oneself under the control of the world. The Word of God clearly instructs: "Be ye not unequally yoked together with unbelievers: for what fellowship hath righteousness with unrighteousness? and what communion hath light with darkness? and what concord hath Christ with Belial? or what part hath he that believeth with an infidel? And what agreement hath the temple of God with idols? for ye are the temple of the living God; as God hath said, I will dwell in them, and walk in them; and I will be their God, and they shall be my people. Wherefore come out from among them, and be ye separate, saith the Lord, and touch not the unclean thing; and I will receive you, and will be a Father unto you, and ye shall be my sons and daughters, saith the Lord Almighty" (II Cor. 6:14-18). Whether it is a matter of theological liberalism or participating in sin, the believer is never to compromise with the world.

Judah's Plan

While Joseph was yet in the pit, his brothers "lifted up their eyes and looked, and, behold, a company of Ishmeelites came from Gilead with their camels bearing spicery and balm and myrrh, going to carry it down to Egypt" (Gen. 37:25).

Judah then thought of a plan. He said to his brothers, "What profit is it if we slay our brother, and conceal his blood? Come, and let us sell him to the Ishmeelites, and let not our hand be upon him; for he is our brother and our flesh. And his brethren were content. Then there passed by Midianites merchantmen; and they drew and lifted up Joseph out of the pit, and sold Joseph to the Ishmeelites for twenty pieces of silver: and they brought Joseph into Egypt" (vv. 26-28).

Judah's plan, to which the brothers agreed, was to avoid the sin of murder but to get rid of Joseph by selling him as a slave, thus making some profit on the side. What a small amount—20 pieces of silver! Think of how little value the brothers placed on Joseph's life. They shrank from killing Joseph but not from enslaving him. This is the kind of honor you find among thieves; even when life is spared, there is little value placed on it.

Circumstances seemed to be on the side of the brothers. This teacl.es us that we need to beware when circumstances seem to favor our will. It is too easy to pay more attention to circumstances than to what God desires.

The hardness of Joseph's brothers was seen in that they permitted him to live but they did not care what the circumstances of his life would be. The hardness of their hearts was in great contrast to the anguish of soul that Joseph was having. That Joseph was experiencing great anguish is seen from a statement his brothers made later: "We saw the anguish of his soul, when he besought us, and we would not hear" (Gen. 42:21).

Note the moral standards of Joseph's brothers. They considered it evil to kill their own brother but permissible to sell him into slavery. Men often substitute their own standards of morality for God's standards. The hardness of their hearts caused them to be insensitive to sin. Man's discernment is tainted by his evil nature. The Book of Romans tells us, "There is none righteous, no, not one: there is none that understandeth, there is none that seeketh after God. They are all gone out of the way, they are together become unprofitable; there is none that doeth good, no, not one" (3:10-12).

Sin and Grace Contrasted

In Acts 7:9 Stephen referred to this incident: "The patriarchs, moved with envy [jealousy], sold Joseph into Egypt: but God was with him." This sets before us the contrast between man's sin and God's grace. As was the case of Joseph's brothers, most of man's trouble stems from his envy or jealousy of others. Even as Christians, we are jealous of others. We envy others because of their prosperity, their position in life, or the recognition they receive. Envy destroys peace and causes dissatisfaction. The Word of God says, "For where envying and strife is, there is confusion and every evil work" (James 3:16). Because of the envy in the hearts of Joseph's brothers, they got rid of Joseph. They thought this was the end of their problems, but it was really only the beginning. Their jealousy of him was later going to bring them great humiliation.

The brothers sold Joseph into Egypt, "but God was with him" (Acts 7:9). In spite of what the unrighteous may do to the child of God, they can proceed no further than God permits. In the midst of such trials, the believer needs to put into practice what is stated in Psalm 37. Although this psalm was not available to Joseph, he was able to put its principles into practice. The first seven verses of this psalm set forth both the negative and positive reactions of believers in the midst of difficulties. Negatively, the believer is told, "Fret not thyself because of evildoers, neither be thou envious against the workers of iniquity" (v. 1). The believer is not to envy because the evil workers will "soon be cut down like the grass, and wither as the green herb" (v. 2). Positively, the believer is to "trust" (v. 3), "delight" (v. 4), "commit" (v. 5), and "rest" (v. 7). Because Joseph put these principles into practice, he was able to be at peace in the midst of overwhelming circumstances.

Joseph took the positive approach and committed everything to God; therefore, the result could only be progress. At first, things seemed to get worse, but even this was used to bring about progress in God's ultimate purpose for him. God overruled the sin of Joseph's brothers in order to accomplish His purpose through Joseph. It is impossible to bring good out of evil, but good can be brought about in spite of evil. The Apostle Paul made it clear to the Christians at Rome that we are never to say, "Let us do evil, that good may come" (Rom. 3:8).

Some refer to Jacob's stealing the birthright and, because he was supposed to have it, as well as the blessing, they cannot see that he was wrong in doing so. But to condone what Jacob did is to make God a partner in evil. Jacob did not have to steal in order to get the birthright and blessing. Also, God did not permit him to possess the blessing for 30 years after he stole the birthright. Jacob possessed the benefits when God's time was right and when he became right with God.

In Joseph's case, although his brothers sinned against him, God was able to bring about good because Joseph dared to follow Him. In effect, Joseph's brothers said, "We'll get rid of Joseph and then we'll see what will become of his dreams." Little did they know how God would teach them severe lessons through what would become of Joseph's dreams.

The Brothers' Lie

After the brothers sold Joseph to the Ishmaelites, Reuben returned to the pit. When he found Joseph was gone, he tore his clothes. He went to his brothers and said, "The child is not; and I, whither shall I go?" (Gen. 37:30). Reuben was concerned that he would be blamed. Even in this he was more concerned for himself than about what had actually happened to Joseph. To cover their sin the brothers "took Joseph's coat, and killed a kid of the goats, and dipped the coat in the blood; and they sent the coat of many colours, and they brought it to their father; and said, This have we found: know now whether it be thy son's coat or no. And he knew it, and said, It is my son's coat; an evil beast hath devoured him; Joseph is without doubt rent in pieces. And Jacob rent his clothes, and put sackcloth upon his loins, and mourned for his son many days" (vv. 31-34).

So deep was Jacob's grief over the apparent death of Joseph, that he refused to be comforted. "All his sons and all his daughters rose up to comfort him; but he refused to be comforted; and he said, For I will go down into the grave unto my son mourning. Thus his father wept for him" (v. 35).

There may be some who would say that the brothers did not actually lie to Jacob—they merely showed him the blood-soaked garment and he drew his own conclusion. But as far as God was concerned it was a lie because their intent was to deceive their father. Although we may not lie by the actual words we speak, it is possible to lie by giving the wrong impression or purposely letting a person draw the wrong conclusion.

Notice that there are no limits to the cruelty of Satan. The brothers evidenced no shame for their sin and even tried to comfort their father. Imagine their trying to comfort him when they were the ones who were responsible for his grief. Although the brothers had apparently gotten rid of Joseph, they had not gotten rid of their responsibility. The Word of God says, "He that covereth his sins shall not prosper: but whoso confesseth and forsaketh them shall have mercy" (Prov. 28:13). God's Word also says, "Be sure your sin will find you out" (Num. 32:23).

Not only is it wrong to murder a person, but it is also wrong to murder the character of a person. How the Lord must be grieved that so much of this is done, even by Christians. Some think they are doing God a service by murdering the character of others, but their sin will find them out.

No sin is single in its consequences. The sin of jealousy led Joseph's brothers from one sin to another. At first they considered murdering Joseph, then they sold him into slavery, then they had to lie to cover their sin, and then they willfully brought deep grief to their father. Consider also their terrible sin of hiding the truth all those years. They were to have great remorse as a result. They must have had great misgivings whenever anything went wrong. The conviction and guilt of their sin was always with them. Though haunted by their guilt, they would not confess their sin to God nor to their father.

Conscience follows a person all his life—even into hell, where it will forever haunt the unbeliever. Luke 16:27,28 reveals that even after the unbeliever has passed from this life he will be able to remember the things of earth. Especially will such a person remember the opportunities he had to receive Christ as Saviour, but he rejected them all.

From this account, we should realize the uncertainty of life itself. Joseph went on a mission but he never returned—he never saw his homeland again. He was mightily used of God in the path in which God led him, but the opportunity to be a blessing in his own land was never his again. Let us take advantage of every opportunity to be a blessing to others.

Life itself is uncertain. Tomorrow we may be in eternity. Are you ready to meet God? You cannot be sure of tomorrow, so take advantage of the opportunity to receive Christ today. God's Word tells us, "Now is the accepted time; behold, now is the day of salvation" (II Cor. 6:2). If God is speaking to you, do not harden your heart but receive Jesus Christ as your Saviour.

Chapter 3

Joseph in Egypt

Joseph, having been sold by his brothers to the Ishmaelites for 20 pieces of silver, "was brought down to Egypt; and Potiphar, an officer of Pharaoh, captain of the guard, an Egyptian, bought him of the hands of the Ishmeelites, which had brought him down thither" (Gen. 39:1).

Think of the questions that must have filled Joseph's mind at this time. He must have thought of the dreams he had had and of how they had indicated that he would someday rule. But now he was nothing more than a slave in a foreign land.

Some, in less serious circumstances, have disbelieved God and have become spiritually shipwrecked. However, Joseph's confidence was not in his ability to understand his circumstances—his confidence was in God.

Joseph dared to believe God. He was committed to the principle which the Apostle Paul later stated to the Christians in Rome: "And we know that all things work together for good to them that love God, to them who are the called according to his purpose" (Rom. 8:28). In the account of Joseph's life, there is no hint that he had any reservations about the fact that God was able to work out His perfect will in his life.

The Word of God says that although Joseph was only a slave in Potiphar's house, "the Lord was with Joseph, and he was a prosperous man" (Gen. 39:2). What a contrast—the slave was a prosperous man! It is character that counts. When

31

a person is in right relationship with God, he is prosperous regardless of his material possessions.

Joseph's character was developed by what he suffered. He was taken from a pit in Dothan and was transferred to the pit of slavery in Egypt. Although his circumstances were even worse, Joseph had a quiet spirit of submission to God. Though he could not see God's plan, he submitted to His will in the things that were happening. Joseph did not question the sovereignty of God. He left the outcome to God and he gave himself to the work at hand. His confidence in God was so complete that he did not have to be concerned about the future but was concerned about doing his work in a way that would bring honor to God.

The key to his life was expressed later when Pharaoh commented to his servants about Joseph: "Can we find such a one as this is, a man in whom the spirit of God is?" (41:38). This was the secret of Joseph's life—he was indwelt by the Spirit of God.

In Old Testament times the Holy Spirit came upon people to empower them for service, but not every believer was indwelt by the Holy Spirit. However, since the coming of the Spirit on the Day of Pentecost, every believer has possessed the indwelling Holy Spirit. Therefore, as a believer you can glorify God, just as Joseph did, regardless of your circumstances. You do not have to ask for any further indwelling or special power, but rather as you yield to the indwelling Spirit, the life of Christ and the power of God will be expressed through your life. Thus the Apostle Paul could say, "I am [have been] crucified with Christ: nevertheless I live; yet not I, but Christ liveth in me: and the life which I now live in the flesh I live by the faith [faithfulness] of the Son of God, who loved me, and gave himself for me" (Gal. 2:20), or, as Paul wrote to the believers at Colossae, "Christ in you, the hope of glory" (Col. 1:27). Remember these tremendous truths. The same Christ who lived a perfect life is indwelling every believer by the Holy Spirit. As we yield to the working and control of the Holy Spirit in our lives, the life of Christ will be manifested through us.

Simply Trusting

One of the great lessons that Joseph learned in Egypt was the lesson of obedience through suffering. He did not understand the mysterious circumstances, but he allowed God to be his circumstances. Because of this, God also became his basic environment—Joseph lived in the sphere of the spiritual even though he was a slave in the house of Potiphar. There was idolatry and corruption all around him, but Joseph was able to remain sensitive to sin and to grow even stronger in his confidence in God because his attention was fixed on God.

We must realize the importance of relying on God to direct our lives, because we do not have the wisdom to know the way we should go. Jeremiah said, "O Lord, I know that the way of man is not in himself: it is not in man that walketh to direct his steps" (Jer. 10:23). Because of His wisdom and omnipotence, God can use even the enemy to carry out His purpose. Our responsibility is to trust Him completely and follow Him wherever He leads. When we commit our way to the Lord and trust in Him, "He shall bring it to pass" (Ps. 37:5). Or, as God inspired Solomon to write, "The preparations of the heart in man, and the answer of the tongue, is from the Lord. All the ways of a man are clean in his own eyes; but the Lord weigheth the spirits. Commit thy works unto the Lord, and thy thoughts shall be established. The Lord hath made all things for himself: yea, even the wicked for the day of evil" (Prov. 16:1-4). Even in the midst of adverse conditions, we need to remember that God is sovereign and will work out His plan through us as we yield to Him.

Joseph was only 17 years of age, but because of his simple trust in God, he performed his duties as a slave to the utmost of his power. He was indwelt by the Spirit; therefore, it was God's power that gave him the ability he needed. Instead of complaining, Joseph faithfully served as a slave. This was because he was serving not just a Gentile master—he was serving God.

Joseph Prospers

Joseph's life of faithfulness was obvious to Potiphar. God's Word says that Joseph's "master saw that the Lord was with him, and that the Lord made all that he did to prosper in his hand" (Gen. 39:3). Even unbelievers are able to discern the Spirit-filled laborer. Do those who work closely with you see your faithfulness and observe that God is spiritually prospering your life?

Sometimes we think what we are doing is so insignificant it is unimportant whether we are faithful in our duties or not. However, the Word of God tells us, "He that is faithful in that which is least is faithful also in much: and he that is unjust in the least is unjust also in much. If therefore ye have not been faithful in the unrighteous mammon [money], who will commit to your trust the true riches? And if ye have not been faithful in that which is another man's, who shall give you that which is your own?" (Luke 16:10-12). The principle the Lord follows in giving rewards is found in Luke 19:17: "And he said unto him, Well, thou good servant: because thou hast been faithful in a very little, have thou authority over ten cities."

Because Potiphar discerned that God was causing Joseph to prosper, "Joseph found grace in his sight, and he served him: and he made him overseer over his house, and all that he had put into his hand. And it came to pass from the time that he had made him overseer in his house, and over all that he had, that the Lord blessed the Egyptian's house for Joseph's sake; and the blessing of the Lord was upon all that he had in the house, and in the field" (Gen. 39:4,5).

Potiphar was being blessed because of Joseph's relationship with God; therefore, he put Joseph in complete charge of his house. So completely did Potiphar trust Joseph that "he left all that he had in Joseph's hand; and he knew not ought he had, save the bread which he did eat. And Joseph was a goodly person, and well favoured" (v. 6).

Even though the believer's greatest reward for having trusted in the Lord is received in eternity, Joseph's life demonstrates that the believer also reaps many rewards during his lifetime. Because of Joseph's trust in God and his desire to please Him in everything he did, Potiphar gave him a better position and an opportunity to have an even wider influence for God. All of this was a further indication that God was with Joseph. He prospered because he was looking to God, not just at the circumstances. Joseph's prosperity was especially a spiritual prosperity, for his testimony had a far greater outreach. Prosperity can never be guaranteed by circumstances alone. Throughout the world men are attempting to create better circumstances because they think that better circumstances will produce better people. But this is not so. People are what they are because of their relationship with God, which is expressed in their faithfulness in whatever they do. Whenever people come into right relationship with God they become better people, which results in better circumstances and environment. The man who is genuinely prosperous lives with his hope in God, not with his eyes fixed on the things of the world.

The way Joseph met his difficulties revealed his godly character and guaranteed his future well-being. Joseph could have given up in hopeless despair, but even as an Old Testament believer he realized he should "not be weary in well doing: for in due season we shall reap, if we faint not" (Gal. 6:9). In Joseph's life we also see the principles stated in I Peter 5: "Humble yourselves therefore under the mighty hand of God, that he may exalt you in due time: casting all your care upon him; for he careth for you. . . . The God of all grace, who hath called us unto his eternal glory by Christ Jesus, after that ye have suffered awhile, make you perfect, stablish, strengthen, settle you" (vv. 6,7,10).

When adversity strikes we should not give up, but we should go to the Word of God where our faith will be strengthened as we see what God is seeking to accomplish through our lives. Our need is to learn to know God better. Then we will be able to say with Jeremiah, "It is of the Lord's mercies that we are not consumed, because his compassions fail not. They are new every morning: great is thy faithfulness. The Lord is my portion, saith my soul; therefore will I hope in him. For the Lord will not cast off for ever: but though he cause grief, yet will he have compassion according to the multitude of his mercies. For he doth not afflict willingly nor grieve the children of men. Wherefore doth a living man complain, a man for the punishment of his sins? Let us search and try our ways, and turn again to the Lord. Let us lift up our heart with our hands unto God in the heavens" (Lam. 3:22-24,31-33,39-41).

Were it not for the mercies of God, you and I would not be able to stand for a minute. This is the thing we need to learn, and it is the thing that Joseph was learning as a young man in Egypt. Potiphar noted there was a difference between Joseph and the other slaves. Potiphar observed from the characteristics of Joseph's life that he had a walk with God. When a person walks closely with God, it is evident even to unbelievers.

The Test of the Body

While in the home of Potiphar, Joseph faced a second test. The first was the test of adversity concerning his home and his brothers. But now came the test of the body when he was allured by Potiphar's wife.

The Word of God says, "It came to pass after these things, that his master's wife cast her eyes upon Joseph; and she said, Lie with me" (Gen. 39:7). Sexual attraction is perhaps the strongest lure of mankind. Whether or not it is controlled can either make or break a person.

Joseph had been presenting a pure, clear-cut testimony for God, and at this time Satan attempted to bring an end to the glory God was receiving through Joseph. This was at a time in Joseph's life when sexual temptation would have been especially hard to resist. However, God had made clear through the dreams He had given to Joseph that Joseph was destined to become a great ruler of some kind. Therefore, Joseph had to keep himself free from the pleasures of sin. Just like Moses of a later time, Joseph was to be the emancipator for the people of Israel—the descendants of Jacob. Moses came to a time when he had to choose, by faith, between the pleasures of sin in Egypt and the hardships with his people. The divine testimony concerning Moses is: "By faith Moses, when he was come to years, refused to be called the son of Pharaoh's daughter; choosing rather to suffer affliction with the people of God, than to enjoy the pleasures of sin for a season" (Heb. 11:24,25).

Joseph was manly and physically attractive. Genesis 39:6 says that "Joseph was a goodly person, and well favoured." One translation renders this to say that Joseph had "beauty of form and face." Doubtlessly he had a good physique, and if he were living today we would say he was the "athletic type." His character and physique made him attractive to Potiphar's wife, and suddenly Joseph found himself facing the most subtle and volcanic temptation of his life.

It is important to remember that Joseph was Potiphar's property. For this reason, Potiphar's wife perhaps thought she could do with this chattel as she liked. Humanly speaking, Joseph could have been very flattered that he was being tempted by his master's wife. What a feeling of importance Joseph might have had!

But Joseph loved God and did not want to do anything that would dishonor Him. This incident shows us, however, that even a believer is not able to build a wall around him high enough to keep out temptation. It is not sin to be tempted; it only becomes sin when one yields to the temptation. Joseph was at the time of life when his reaction to temptation would have lasting effects. If he had yielded to the temptation of Potiphar's wife, who can imagine the different course that history might have taken.

What a person accepts or rejects, particularly in the realm of sexual temptation, will affect the rest of his life. This is why God's Word says, "Keep thy heart with all diligence; for out of it are the issues of life" (Prov. 4:23). The Apostle Paul solemnly charged young Timothy: "Flee also youthful lusts: but follow righteousness, faith, charity [love], peace, with them that call on the Lord out of a pure heart" (II Tim. 2:22).

Think how easy it would have been for Joseph to have yielded to the temptation of Potiphar's wife. He was a long way from home and no one would probably know about his sin. He was living in a hopeless situation as a slave and was apart from all godly influence, so there was little to strengthen him against temptation. He had none of the helps to a holy life that we have—neither the Bible nor books which offer the counsel of godly men. In Joseph's situation—being tempted by the words, looks and actions of Potiphar's wife—he was able to resist only because he was indwelt by the Spirit.

Characteristics of Joseph's Temptation

There are several things to observe about the temptation which Joseph faced: It was totally unexpected. It came at a time when everything was going well for Joseph. God was blessing him—and his master, Potiphar, was being blessed because of him.

Also, the temptation came from an unexpected source. As Joseph was active in the routine of his duties, he never dreamed he would come face to face with one of the greatest temptations of his life. Because it was so unexpected, he had no time to strengthen himself against the temptation.

We need to be aware that temptation is not predictable; it strikes as lightning. It never waits for us to put on the armor so we will be able to resist it. This is why we need to be wearing the armor at all times and be prepared for temptation. This is why the Apostle Paul wrote: "Wherefore take unto you the whole armour of God, that ye may be able to withstand in the evil day" (Eph. 6:13). Just as Joseph did not know when he would be tempted, neither do we. We must be prepared.

When Potiphar's wife asked Joseph to lie with her, "He refused, and said unto his master's wife, Behold, my master wotteth [knoweth] not what is with me in the house, and he hath committed all that he hath to my hand; there is none greater in this house than I; neither hath he kept back any thing from me but thee, because thou art his wife: how then can I do this great wickedness, and sin against God?" (Gen. 39:8,9).

The temptation was extremely difficult to resist because Potiphar's wife did not give up. She spoke to Joseph about it "day by day" (v. 10). However, "he hearkened not unto her, to lie by her, or to be with her" (v. 10). If Joseph were living in our day of the new morality, he would find that many would laugh at him for his beliefs. They would say, "After all, young people have to sow their wild oats, they have to experience sin in order to appreciate what is good." The Apostle Paul answered this kind of argument when he said, "Be not deceived; God is not mocked: for whatsoever a man soweth, that shall he also reap" (Gal. 6:7).

Joseph was able to resist the continual temptation of Potiphar's wife because he took a strong stand against it from the very first. If he had even considered the possibility of committing fornication with Potiphar's wife when she first tempted him, he would have been easy prey later on. But the indwelling Spirit helped Joseph to steadfastly resist the first temptation. By a definite act of Joseph's will he refused to yield to what he knew was sin.

Once we have said No to sin, it is easier to reject it the next time. But though there be pleasure in sin for a season (Heb. 11:25), as Christians we must determine that we will not yield to the temptation of sin and bring dishonor to God, as well as make shipwreck of our own lives. When we say No to sin and Yes to Christ, the indwelling Holy Spirit will empower us to carry out our decision. The Word of God says, "Walk in the Spirit, and ye shall not fulfil the lust of the flesh" (Gal. 5:16).

Another factor in Joseph's temptation that would have made it especially hard to resist was the favorable opportunity. "It came to pass about this time, that Joseph went into the house to do his business; and there was none of the men of the house there within" (Gen. 39:11). The Devil always selects the most opportune time to cast his darts. None of the men were in the house, and Joseph could easily have reasoned that no one would ever find out. But Joseph's faith in God kept him from being victimized by the darts of Satan. Paul stated this truth in the New Testament: "Above all, taking the shield of faith, wherewith ye shall be able to quench all the fiery darts of the wicked [the evil one]" (Eph. 6:16).

The time to take the shield of faith and be sure it is securely in place is early in the morning during your devotional time. As you prepare for the day's activities, be sure your heart is right with God and that your dependence is on Him. The time in the morning spent alone with God is the most important time of the day for you.

Joseph's temptation offered another great inducement to yield. This was Joseph's opportunity to get in good standing with his master's wife. With her influence on her husband, Joseph could have reasoned, this could have provided an excellent opportunity for advancement. But he shut his eyes to worldly advantage and clung to the moral principles which God had instilled in him. Joseph's response was, "How then can I do this great wickedness, and sin against God?" (Gen. 39:9). Joseph's ambition to be in good standing with God overshadowed all the worldly advantages. He was motivated by principle—not by expediency. Only a God-indwelt young man could have continued to resist.

So, too, every believer today has Christ living within him. The Son of God, who never sinned, is in us to live His life through us. The power of sin over us has been broken by the death of Christ on the cross. We do not have to yield to its power. Being indwelt by the Holy Spirit, we are fully able to say No to sin and Yes to Christ.

Potiphar had perfect faith in Joseph. The perfect faith of the master called for perfect faithfulness on the part of the servant. But far above this, duty to God reigned supreme in Joseph's life.

To Joseph, God was always first. Even though others might never learn of an act of fornication with Potiphar's wife, he realized it would dishonor God; therefore, he would not even consider it. We, too, need to remember that even if no one else sees us commit an act of sin, God sees. It is impossible to hide anything from Him.

Joseph Successfully Resists

As far as Joseph was concerned, his stand was firm against temptation. He realized his body was "not for fornication, but for the Lord." In our age of loose morals, we need to weigh carefully the words of I Corinthians 6:13-20: "Meats for the belly, and the belly for meats: but God shall destroy both it and them. Now the body is not for fornication, but for the Lord; and the Lord for the body. And God hath both raised up the Lord, and will also raise up us by his own power. Know ye not that your bodies are the members of Christ? shall I then take the members of Christ, and make them the members of an harlot? God forbid. What? know ye not that he which is joined to an harlot is one body? for two, saith he, shall be one flesh. But he that is joined unto the Lord is one spirit. Flee fornication. Every sin that a man doeth is without the body; but he that committeth fornication sinneth against his own body. What? know ye not that your body is the temple of the Holy Ghost which is in you, which ye have of God, and ye are not your own? For ye are bought with a price: therefore glorify God in your body, and in your spirit, which are God's."

In the above verses we have the unequivocal command, "Flee fornication." Regardless of what the proponents of situation ethics try to tell us, God's Word makes it clear that there is no possibility of fornication ever being acceptable. Notice also from this passage that the strongest argument Paul used against the believer's ever committing fornication was not the possibility of pregnancy nor the possibility of venereal disease but that the Christian's body belongs to the Lord. The Holy Spirit indwells every believer; therefore, the believer's body is referred to as the "temple of the Holy Ghost." To the Apostle Paul, it was unbelievable that any

Christian would want to take the temple of the Holy Spirit and use it to commit an act of fornication.

Joseph determined to use his body to glorify God instead of using it as an instrument of fornication. When he refused Potiphar's wife again, "she caught him by his garment, saying, Lie with me: and he left his garment in her hand, and fled, and got him out" (Gen. 39:12). Joseph knew it was better to lose his garment than to lose his purity and pure conscience. He did not linger in the presence of temptation—he fled.

Flight is the only safety for certain forms of temptation. We are told to meet some temptations head on: "Submit yourselves therefore to God. Resist the devil, and he will flee from you" (James 4:7). But other temptations can be resisted only by flight. To linger and toy with temptation is to fall. Someone has said, "Kill the serpent; don't stroke him."

Many temptations come against the body, but the positive action the believer is to take is clearly stated in Romans 12:1,2: "I beseech you therefore, brethren, by the mercies of God, that ye present your bodies a living sacrifice, holy, acceptable unto God, which is your reasonable service. And be not conformed to this world: but be ye transformed by the renewing of your mind, that ye may prove what is that good, and acceptable, and perfect, will of God."

Whereas "sacrifice" always speaks of death, Paul said the believer's body is to be a "living" sacrifice. The believer needs to recognize that he is dead to sin but alive to God. Notice also in this passage that the believer is to be transformed by the renewing of his mind. The mind is used to make decisions. As the believer spends time in God's Word and in fellowship with God in prayer, his mind will be renewed so he will desire that which is right and will make the proper decisions.

Lessons About Temptation

Concerning sexual temptations such as Joseph faced, there are several important things we need to remember.

First, sexual desire in itself is not sinful. Along with the other natural physical desires, God has given us a sexual desire. The individual is personally responsible to control this desire God has given him, but the desire itself is not bad.

Second, temptation in itself is not sinful. This is obvious because Jesus "was in all points tempted like as we are, yet without sin" (Heb. 4:15). Temptation can lead to sin, but it becomes sin only when we harbor it and go on to gratify the lust of the flesh.

Third, we cannot depend on God's help if we deliberately walk into temptation. There is no indication that Joseph was in the house other than when he had duties to perform there. Genesis 39:11 says that "Joseph went into the house to do his business. . . ." He was careful not to be in the presence of Potiphar's wife except when he absolutely had to be.

We should not expect God to give us strength to overcome temptation if we willfully and enjoyably walk in the area of temptation. Joseph could claim God's help immediately because he was caught off guard when Potiphar's wife became insistent and "caught him by his garment" (v. 12). Joseph did the only thing he could in the situation—he fled. He immediately got out of the area of temptation.

Joseph and David Contrasted

There was a great deal of difference between the way Joseph reacted to temptation and the way King David reacted. The account of David's great sin is given in II Samuel 11:1-4: "And it came to pass, after the year was expired, at the time when kings go forth to battle, that David sent Joab, and his servants with him, and all Israel; and they destroyed the children of Ammon, and besieged Rabbah. But David tarried still at Jerusalem. And it came to pass in an eveningtide, that David arose from off his bed, and walked upon the roof of the king's house: and from the roof he saw a woman washing herself; and the woman was very beautiful to look upon. And David sent and enquired after the woman.

And one said, Is not this Bath-sheba, the daughter of Eliam, the wife of Uriah the Hittite? And David sent messengers, and took her; and she came in unto him, and he lay with her; for she was purified from her uncleanness: and she returned unto her house."

Instead of being out in battle as he should have been, David decided to take it easy and enjoy the pleasures of life. From the rooftop where he had been walking, he saw a beautiful woman washing herself and he sent and asked about her. How different from Joseph! David might have been caught off guard when he first saw the woman, but he harbored the temptation. Instead of fleeing temptation, he took willful steps to learn more about her. Had David done what Joseph did, how different this part of his life story would have been!

Elements of Victory

Consider some of the important factors in Joseph's victory. First, there was his unquestioned loyalty to God. When Potiphar's wife first tempted Joseph, he asked, "How then can I do this great wickedness, and sin against God?" (Gen. 39:9). To Joseph, sin was always against God and was far more serious than crime against man.

Second, although Joseph was now living in a corrupt society, he was still shocked by sin. Others might have looked on his opportunity to commit fornication as "having a little fling," but Joseph saw it as "this great wickedness." We will have victory in our lives only when we see sin as being as awful as it really is.

Third, Joseph won the victory over temptation because he was habitually prepared. When temptation struck, Joseph was walking in fellowship with God. He was living the principle which was recorded later in the New Testament: "Walk in the Spirit, and ye shall not fulfil the lust of the flesh" (Gal. 5:16). Joseph's faith was firmly established in God, and because of this he was able to defend himself against the attacks of Satan. So also the Bible tells Christians,

"Above all, taking the shield of faith, wherewith ye shall be able to quench all the fiery darts of the wicked" (Eph. 6:16). If one waits until after the temptation strikes, there is usually not time to take the shield of faith and ward off the attacks of Satan. This is why the believer must constantly be prepared by having the shield of faith ready at all times. Because of this need, it is impossible for me to emphasize too strongly that you must take time for your devotional life in the morning. This should be a time when you are completely alone with God and His Word. This will give you spiritual strength as you take the armor of God for the day ahead of you.

Fourth, Joseph was able to victoriously stand against temptation because his mind had not been dwelling on sex. Had he been thinking constantly about sex, this would have conditioned him for a fall into sin. But his mind was clear. He was concentrating on his work and not even considering the possibility of yielding to the desires of Potiphar's wife. To Joseph, it was unthinkable to even consider yielding to such a temptation.

Results of Resisting

One would think that Joseph's great moral victory would have resulted in God giving him a significant reward. Instead, there followed even greater calamity. Someone has said, "Hell hath no fury like a woman scorned." Potiphar's wife reacted drastically. Her disappointment in passion turned to hate. She used the garment that Joseph had left behind to make it appear that he was guilty.

"And it came to pass, when she saw that he had left his garment in her hand, and was fled forth, that she called unto the men of her house, and spake unto them, saying, See, he hath brought in an Hebrew unto us to mock us; he came in unto me to lie with me, and I cried with a loud voice: and it came to pass, when he heard that I lifted up my voice and cried, that he left his garment with me, and fled, and got him out. And she laid up his garment by her, until his lord came home. And she spake unto him according to these words, saying, The Hebrew servant, which thou hast brought unto us, came in unto me to mock me: and it came to pass, as I lifted up my voice and cried, that he left his garment with me, and fled out" (Gen. 39:13-18).

What a lie Potiphar's wife told about Joseph! He had refused her invitation to sin because he did not want to dishonor God, and now through her lie God was seemingly being dishonored anyhow.

When Potiphar heard his wife's report, he became very angry. He took Joseph and "put him into the prison, a place where the king's prisoners were bound: and he was there in prison" (v. 20). Could this be the reward Joseph received for his faithfulness to God? How discouraged he might have been. Think of all the things that had happened to him. At home, his brothers had taken his robe, which indicated his birthright, and had cast him into a pit. Then he went through the experience of being sold as a slave and carried to Egypt. Now he was falsely charged and made to look as if he were living in the squalor of sin rather than seeking to bring glory to God. Perhaps Joseph wondered, What next? He may have asked himself, What about those dreams God gave me that indicated I would be a ruler? Does godliness really pay?

Concerning this time in his life, Psalm 105:17-19 says, "He sent a man before them, even Joseph, who was sold for a servant: whose feet they hurt with fetters: he was laid in iron: until the time that his word came: the word of the Lord tried him." Joseph had learned that his body was the Lord's, now he had to learn to commit even his soul-life to God.

In prison—the place of despair—a young man like this would experience more severe doubts than ever. Did God really send those dreams that came to him which indicated that he would be a ruler someday? Or were they just boyhood ambitions? In addition to this doubt, Satan could have tormented Joseph's mind with the thought, "I have been cast off by my family and now by my master to whom I was faithful. I wonder if God has cast me off also?"

Although everything seemed to be going against him, the Bible emphasizes that "the Lord was with Joseph, and showed him mercy, and gave him favour in the sight of the keeper of the prison" (Gen. 39:21). Even though Joseph's situation seemed hopeless, God never left him for one moment.

The Believer's Assurance

We, too, have the assurance of God's Word: "I will never leave thee, nor forsake thee" (Heb. 13:5). In the original language, this phrase is very emphatic: "I will by no means leave you nor will I by any means forsake you." God will never leave us helpless nor abandoned. Therefore, "we may boldly say, The Lord is my helper, and I will not fear what man shall do unto me" (v. 6). Do you have this confidence? Regardless of how adverse your circumstances are, as a Christian do you know that God will never desert you?

Notice how David prayed in the time of trouble: "I called upon the Lord in distress: the Lord answered me, and set me in a large place. The Lord is on my side; I will not fear: what can man do unto me? The Lord taketh my part with them that help me: therefore shall I see my desire upon them that hate me. It is better to trust in the Lord than to put confidence in man. It is better to trust in the Lord than to put confidence in princes" (Ps. 118:5-9).

Psalm 56 is especially dear to me because I have gone to it many times when I have been maligned by others. The Psalmist said, "Be merciful unto me, O God: for man would swallow me up; he fighting daily oppresseth me. Mine enemies would daily swallow me up: for they be many that fight against me, O thou most High. What time I am afraid, I will trust in thee. In God have I put my trust: I will not be afraid what man can do unto me. Thy vows are upon me, O God: I will render praises unto thee. For thou hast delivered my soul from death: wilt not thou deliver my feet from falling, that I may walk before God in the light of the living?" (vv. 1-3,11-13). The Christian can come to God and thank Him for salvation and then pray that God will cause him to walk in the path he should and will keep his feet from falling. This is the kind of prayer that I imagine Joseph was praying in prison.

Joseph was victorious in testing because he was indwelt by the Spirit. Every believer during the Church Age is also indwelt by the Holy Spirit and can be confident of victory when he relies on the Spirit's control. We believers have no reason to fail. We may take confidence in the benediction of Hebrews 13:20,21: "Now the God of peace, that brought again from the dead our Lord Jesus, that great shepherd of the sheep, through the blood of the everlasting covenant, make you perfect in every good work to do his will, working in you that which is wellpleasing in his sight, through Jesus Christ; to whom be glory for ever and ever. Amen."

Several other passages of Scripture give us confidence in the time of testing: I Corinthians 15:57: "But thanks be to God, which giveth us the victory through our Lord Jesus Christ"; II Corinthians 2:14: "Now thanks be unto God, which always causeth us to triumph in Christ, and maketh manifest the savour of his knowledge by us in every place"; I John 5:4,5: "For whatsoever is born of God overcometh the world: and this is the victory that overcometh the world, even our faith. Who is he that overcometh the world, but he that believeth that Jesus is the Son of God?"

Do you have the triumph spoken of in these verses? Do you have the victory that God has made possible for you? Jesus Christ indwells the believer to bring about victory in his life.

Perhaps you have been going through circumstances that seem as hopeless to you as Joseph's did to him. If so, you have probably realized that your faith is weak and faltering. However, you must have confidence, not in your faith, but in the faithfulness of the Son of God. The Apostle Paul said, "I am [have been] crucified with Christ: nevertheless I live; yet not I, but Christ liveth in me: and the life which I now live in the flesh I live by the faith [faithfulness] of the Son of God, who loved me, and gave himself for me" (Gal. 2:20). Joseph had passed the test of adversity brought on by his brothers and the test of the body brought on by Potiphar's wife. Although he had been victorious, he became a victim of his brothers' hatred and of false accusations made by Potiphar's wife. But it is wonderful to see from Joseph's life that he realized he did not *have* to sin under any condition. Nor do we have to yield to Satan's temptations. We can be morally pure and victorious over sin regardless of what those around us are doing. The One who empowered Joseph is the same One who empowers us, for Christ is "the same yesterday, and to day, and for ever" (Heb. 13:8).

Chapter 4

Joseph in Prison

Joseph in Prison

Because Potiphar's wife could not get Joseph to yield to her wishes, she framed Joseph on a morals charge and he was cast into prison. Later, the psalmist recorded: "He sent a man before them, even Joseph, who was sold for a servant. His feet they hurt with fetters, he was laid in chains of iron and his soul entered into the iron; until his word [to his cruel brothers] came true, the word of the Lord tried and tested him. The king sent and loosed him, even the ruler of the peoples, and let him go free" (Ps. 105:17-20, Amp.).

The Test of the Soul

Having been thrown into prison on a false charge, Joseph began to experience another great test in his life. Previously he had experienced the test of adversity when he was hated by his brothers and sold into Egypt as a slave. Then he had experienced the test of his body when Potiphar's wife appealed to his sexual desires. Now he faced the test of his soul. This was a mental test because in the soul lies the intellect, emotions and will. Satan had not been able to defeat Joseph by an attack on the desires of his body, so now Satan attacked Joseph's mind.

The iron that held Joseph physically was not as much of a problem as the iron that was attempting to hold him mentally. He had passed the test of the body with glowing

50

colors, but the test of the soul was an even more severe test. Joseph had learned that the Lord was the owner of his body and the director of all circumstances; now he had to learn to discern between the mind of self and the mind of the Spirit. It was necessary for him to make God the God of his soul-life—of his mind, emotions and will. In order for Him to use Joseph, God had to be in charge of every area of his life.

Did Joseph doubt the authenticity of his boyhood dreams? He had reason to do so, and perhaps he was now wondering how he could prove that those dreams were of God and not of his own youthful ambitious desires.

There is no record that he said anything in self-defense as he was cast into prison. There was only silence. Why did he not say something? Why did he not defend himself against such a despicable charge? Apparently, Joseph determined that he was not going to bring a division between his master and his wife in order to save himself. Even in this we see how noble Joseph was. He refused to defend himself at someone else's expense. There was no recrimination, only a quiet endurance of wrong.

The Scriptures tell us, "For this is thankworthy, if a man for conscience toward God endure grief, suffering wrongfully. For what glory is it, if, when ye be buffeted for your faults, ye shall take it patiently? but if, when ye do well, and suffer for it, ye take it patiently, this is acceptable with God" (I Pet. 2:19,20).

The prison that Joseph was in was not a prison as we normally think of one, with proper lighting and circulation. It was most likely only a hole in the ground. Several years ago I visited the spot where Paul was supposedly imprisoned in Rome. It was a cold, damp and dark hole. It was in such a place that Joseph found himself because of the accusation of Potiphar's wife.

Joseph might have thought, "Didn't I obey my father instead of being like my wicked brothers? But what has it profited me—nothing. All I experienced was the murderous jealousy and hatred of my brothers."

Joseph might also have reflected on how he had resisted physical temptation and thought, "Didn't I fully resist the temptation of Potiphar's wife because I didn't want to sin against God? And what has it gained me—nothing." Joseph was now in prison with a stigma as bad as if he had actually committed sin.

Comfort in Prison

Although humanly speaking there was only despair for Joseph, the Word of God emphasizes, "But the Lord was with Joseph, and showed him mercy, and gave him favour in the sight of the keeper of the prison" (Gen. 39:21). The Lord had been with Joseph in the palace of Potiphar—even in the midst of temptation—and the Lord was with Joseph in prison. Regardless of the change of circumstances, Joseph was able to remain in complete fellowship with God because he faced sin squarely. God did not send Joseph to prison; He went with him.

As Christians, we also should take comfort in God's words, "I will never leave thee, nor forsake thee. So that we may boldly say, The Lord is my helper, and I will not fear what man shall do unto me" (Heb. 13:5,6). Even though union is never broken, communion can be broken. That which breaks our fellowship with God is sin. But I John 1:7 assures us, "If we walk in the light, as he is in the light, we have fellowship one with another, and the blood of Jesus Christ his Son cleanseth us from all sin." Whenever the believer's fellowship has been broken through sin, it can be restored only through confession: "If we confess our sins, he [God] is faithful and just to forgive us our sins, and to cleanse us from all unrighteousness" (I John 1:9).

Joseph was walking in the light—walking with God—even though the path took him into prison. Although there was physical darkness around him, he was in the midst of spiritual light—nothing was able to sever his relationship with God.

When we are absorbed with God, all places and experiences are much the same. Some of you are experiencing turmoil of soul. Could it be because you are concentrating more on your circumstances than you are on God? Note what the psalmist said, "Whither shall I go from thy spirit? or whither shall I flee from thy presence? If I ascend up into heaven, thou art there: if I make my bed in hell, behold, thou art there. If I take the wings of the morning, and dwell in the uttermost parts of the sea; even there shall thy hand lead me, and thy right hand shall hold me. If I say, Surely the darkness shall cover me; even the night shall be light about me. Yea, the darkness hideth not from thee; but the night shineth as the day: the darkness and the light are both alike to thee. For thou hast possessed my reins [inward parts]: thou hast covered me in my mother's womb. I will praise thee; for I am fearfully and wonderfully made: marvellous are thy works; and that my soul knoweth right well" (Ps. 139:7-14).

All that the psalmist, David, went through when he was fleeing from Saul, and in his other hardships, could never completely discourage him because he knew that God was with him.

When Paul and Silas were in prison in Philippi they sang praises unto God because they knew He was with them (Acts 16:24-34). While they were singing, God caused—by means of an earthquake—the prison doors to open and everyone's bands to fall off. The keeper of the prison was about to kill himself because he thought the prisoners had fled, but Paul and Silas stopped him from taking his life and were able to lead him and his family to the Lord. We sing, "He giveth me a song in the night," but have you really experienced it?

When John Bunyan was cast into prison for preaching the Word, it seemed like a terrible thing. However, it was while he was in prison that he wrote *Pilgrim's Progress*—one of the greatest books apart from the Bible.

God Will Avenge

There will be times when your words will be misconstrued and your actions will be misunderstood. You will be slandered and falsely accused and even persecuted. When that happens, what will your reaction be? It will depend on your relationship to God. The tendency will be to do what the world does—to justify yourself by maintaining that what others say is not true and even go to court to prove it, if necessary. But that is not the way of God. The believer takes his case to the highest court—the court of heaven—and leaves it before the throne of God: "Casting all your care upon him; for he careth for you" (I Pet. 5:7). The believer depends on God to clear his name. As long as the believer knows he is in fellowship with God, he is content to wait months and, in some cases, years for God to vindicate him. But one thing can be counted on: God's time will come; He will avenge. Hebrews 10:30 says, "Vengeance belongeth unto me, I will recompense, saith the Lord. And again, The Lord shall judge His people."

The believer's responsibility is to commit everything to God to work out as He sees best, not to worry about when God will avenge him. This is so clearly seen in Psalm 37:5,6: "Commit thy way unto the Lord; trust also in him; and he shall bring it to pass. And he shall bring forth thy righteousness as the light, and thy judgment as the noonday." We can afford to wait for God's time; we do not have to attempt to clear ourselves of false accusations.

Since this is true, we need to take seriously Paul's admonition in I Corinthians 4:4,5: "I am not conscious of anything against myself, and I feel blameless; but I am not vindicated and acquitted before God on that account. It is the Lord [Himself] Who examines and judges me. So do not make any hasty or premature judgments before the time when the Lord comes [again], for He will both bring to light the secret things that are (now hidden) in darkness, and disclose and expose the (secret) aims (motives and purposes) of hearts. Then every man will receive his (due) commendation from God" (Amp.). God says He will do it—you can trust Him to do so.

Joseph's Secret

In all of Joseph's troubles, his secret power was in his consciousness of the presence of God. This was the key to Joseph's life, especially while he was in prison.

God is with the believer whether the believer realizes it or not. But the realization of God's presence brings peace and joy. It is only when we realize that God will never leave us nor forsake us that we are content to let Him work out His will in our lives.

God had not forsaken Joseph, even though at times the circumstances might indicate that He had. These were all steps to bring Joseph to the place where God wanted him. God was going to exalt Joseph someday and it was necessary for Joseph to pass through these tests in order that he might be God's man of the hour.

As the Apostle Paul reflected on all that he had gone through or would go through for the Lord Jesus Christ, he said, "But none of these things move me, neither count I my life dear unto myself, so that I might finish my course with joy, and the ministry, which I have received of the Lord Jesus, to testify the gospel of the grace of God" (Acts 20:24). Regardless of what it cost, the Apostle Paul wanted everything God had for him in order that he might finish his course with joy. Paul saw himself as on a course set by God. God has a plan for every person's life. It is important that we find it and that we let God lead us a step at a time in fulfilling His plan.

The Psalmist David said, "You saw me before I was born and scheduled each day of my life before I began to breathe. Every day was recorded in Your Book! How precious it is, Lord, to realize that You are thinking about me constantly! I can't even count how many times a day Your thoughts turn towards me! And when I waken in the morning, You are still thinking of me!" (Ps. 139:16-18, Living Psalms and Proverbs). It was because David was so conscious of God's presence that he could say, "Rest in the Lord, and wait patiently for him" (Ps. 37:7).

Evil may have temporary victories, but remember that they are only temporary. God's will and God's purpose will always prevail. We must wait quietly; we must go forward humbly. We must live faithfully and trust boldly until God justifies all things by His divine intervention and brings glory to His name.

God has much in store for us in the future. Referring to this, the Apostle Paul wrote that "in Christ Jesus He [God] caused us to rise, and He seated us with Him in the heavenly spheres, so that He might show the immeasurable wealth of His grace, which through the future ages His goodness brings to us through Christ Jesus" (Eph. 2:6,7, Berkeley).

Joseph's answer to every question which arose was "God." Joseph steadfastly refused to be unfaithful to his God, no matter what the consequence. In duty he was loyal; in temptation he was strong; in prison he was faithful. The outstanding characteristic of Joseph's life was faithfulness—loyalty to an Almighty God. No matter how difficult the circumstances were, and no matter how low the morals of others around him were, Joseph's strong convictions never let him depart from his loyalty to God.

Someone has said that true independence is acting in the crowd as one thinks in solitude. It is important that we spend time alone with the Word of God, establishing our values before Him. Then when we are in the crowd we should never compromise the values God has brought us to see.

Joseph was faithful to God regardless of the circumstances. The Word of God assures us, "He that is faithful in that which is least is faithful also in much: and he that is unjust in the least is unjust also in much. If therefore ye have not been faithful in the unrighteous mammon [money], who will commit to your trust the true riches? And if ye have not been faithful in that which is another man's, who shall give you that which is your own?" (Luke 16:10-12).

Promotion in Prison

God gave Joseph favor in the eyes of the prison keeper. Like Potiphar, the prison keeper soon discovered that Joseph was a person of unusual quality. The Word of God says that "the keeper of the prison committed to Joseph's hand all the prisoners that were in the prison; and whatsoever they did there, he was the doer of it. The keeper of the prison looked not to any thing that was under his hand; because the Lord was with him, and that which he did, the Lord made it to prosper" (Gen. 39:22,23). Regardless of Joseph's circumstances, his character exposed itself clearly to others. The favor of God on a person's life cannot be concealed. It was evident to the keeper of the prison that Joseph was blessed by God.

Do you have this kind of character? Some confuse character with reputation. What's the difference? Some have said it this way: "Reputation is what others suppose we are; character is what we really are. Reputation is what men think you are; character is what God knows you are. Reputation is what is chiseled on your tombstone; character is what the angels say about you before the throne of God" (*The Cream Book*, p. 59). Which are you more concerned about—character or reputation?

Because Joseph submitted to his adversities, he was mellowed and ennobled by them rather than being embittered by them. Joseph was a living demonstration of the words later recorded in I Peter 2:18-20: "Servants, be subject to your masters with all fear; not only to the good and gentle, but also to the froward. For this is thankworthy, if a man for conscience toward God endure grief, suffering wrongfully. For what glory is it, if, when ye be buffeted for your faults, ye shall take it patiently? but if, when ye do well, and suffer for it, ye take it patiently, this is acceptable with God."

In the following verses, Peter wrote why we, living after the cross, should be willing to suffer in such a way: "For even hereunto were ye called: because Christ also suffered for us, leaving us an example, that ye should follow his steps: who did no sin, neither was guile found in his mouth: who, when he was reviled, reviled not again; when he suffered, he threatened not; but committed himself to him that judgeth righteously" (vv. 21-23). Christ lives *in* us and, if we allow Him, He will live His life *through* us. Our responsibility is to yield to Him so that His will might be performed in us.

The dungeon into which Joseph was cast was no doubt a prison for those connected with royalty. "And it came to pass after these things, that the butler of the king of Egypt and his baker had offended their lord the king of Egypt. And Pharaoh was wroth against two of his officers, against the chief of the butlers, and against the chief of the bakers. And he put them in ward in the house of the captain of the guard, into the prison, the place where Joseph was bound. And the captain of the guard charged Joseph with them, and he served them: and they continued a season in ward" (Gen. 40:1-4).

Willing Service

Service was one of the main links in the remarkable chain of events that God brought about in Joseph's life. Now he was made responsible for the king's butler and baker, for "he served them" (v. 4). Joseph was made responsible for them because his godly character had won him favor with those in authority. And Joseph was willing to serve in any way he could.

Concerning the attitude of service, Matthew 23:10-12 says, "Neither be ye called masters: for one is your Master, even Christ. But he that is greatest among you shall be your servant. And whosoever shall exalt himself shall be abased; and he that shall humble himself shall be exalted." The Lord Jesus Christ Himself said, "He that is greatest among you, let him be as the younger; and he that is chief, as he that doth serve. For whether is greater, he that sitteth at meat, or he that serveth? is not he that sitteth at meat? but I am among you as he that serveth" (Luke 22:26,27). This same Jesus lives in us; therefore, when we let Him have control of our lives we will have the attitude of servants, not masters.

As Joseph faithfully served God by serving others, little did he know how God would use his association with the butler and baker to bring about His will. Because God was in it, the relationship of the Hebrew slave with Pharaoh's two servants had far-reaching results.

We also need to realize that the smallest circumstance of life has meaning. Even though we may not understand how God can use a particular thing to work out His glory, we need to realize that He can use small things as well as big things to accomplish His will. The words, "all things," are very important words in Romans 8:28: "And we know that all things work together for good to them that love God, to them who are the called according to his purpose."

Although the circumstances were extremely difficult in prison, Joseph practiced the same standards of faithfulness there that he had elsewhere. He had learned the secret of suffering uncomplainingly. Because of the strength of his trust in the Lord, Joseph won the victory over self even in prison. He learned obedience by that which he suffered.

Note particularly that Joseph's religious convictions did not stand in the way of earthly promotion. Men of the world soon detect when a person has quality of character. Joseph did not compromise to obtain promotions; the promotions came because he had a character that would not compromise.

Pharaoh's butler and baker "dreamed a dream both of them, each man his dream in one night, each man according to the interpretation of his dream, the butler and the baker of the king of Egypt, which were bound in the prison. And Joseph came in unto them in the morning, and looked upon them, and, behold, they were sad. And he asked Pharaoh's officers that were with him in the ward of his lord's house, saying, Wherefore look ye so sadly to day?" (Gen. 40:5-7).

Notice Joseph's readiness to approach these two officers. Again, it indicates his faithfulness in little things. He observed they were sad, and he remarked about it. He did not wait for some great occasion to express his concern. He was sensitive to little things and was faithful in doing something about them. The Lord's principle of rewarding is that when we are faithful over little He makes us ruler over much. This is clearly seen from Matthew 25:21: "His lord said unto him, Well done, thou good and faithful servant: thou hast been faithful over a few things, I will make thee ruler over many things: enter thou into the joy of thy lord." What kind of position are you going to have when you get to glory? Are you interested today only in the things of importance and thus, do you leave the little things to someone else? If you are faithful in the little things, God will see to it that you are rewarded with even greater responsibility.

When Joseph inquired about why the officers were so sad, "they said unto him, We have dreamed a dream, and there is no interpreter of it. And Joseph said unto them, Do not interpretations belong to God? tell me them, I pray you" (Gen. 40:8).

The butler and the baker were sad because there was no one to interpret their dreams. Joseph would immediately have empathy with these men because he had real reason to doubt his own dreams. He could have seriously wondered if his dreams had been God-given or if they had been only the result of his imagination. If they were of God, why was he now in prison? However, Joseph's confidence in God had not been shaken at all even though he did not understand how God was working out His plan.

Without hesitation, Joseph said to the butler and the baker, "Do not interpretations belong to God?" (v. 8). He invited the butler and the baker to tell him their dreams, with the obvious intent that he would seek God's interpretation of them. He could never have done this if he had harbored secret doubts about his own youthful dreams. But he believed God. He believed that God gave the dreams as well as the interpretation of them. Since there was no Bible in that day, God communicated to men through dreams and visions. Joseph had learned the difference between human thoughts and the thoughts of the Spirit of God within. It is in the mind where the ability to discern spiritual values resides.

Joseph was now being tested in the area of his mind. In prison, Satan attacked his mind and sought to cause him to doubt God's goodness and sovereignty.

The Butler's Dream

The butler told his dream to Joseph: "In my dream, behold, a vine was before me; and in the vine were three branches: and it was as though it budded, and her blossoms shot forth; and the clusters thereof brought forth ripe grapes: and Pharaoh's cup was in my hand: and I took the grapes, and pressed them into Pharaoh's cup, and I gave the cup into Pharaoh's hand" (vv. 9-11).

Having listened to the chief butler's dream, Joseph said to him, "This is the interpretation of it: The three branches are three days: yet within three days shall Pharaoh lift up thine head, and restore thee unto thy place: and thou shalt deliver Pharaoh's cup into his hand, after the former manner when thou wast his butler" (vv. 12,13).

Having assured the chief butler that he would be restored to his former responsibility, Joseph urged him, "But think on me when it shall be well with thee and shew kindness, I pray thee, unto me, and make mention of me unto Pharaoh, and bring me out of this house: for indeed I was stolen away out of the land of the Hebrews: and here also have I done nothing that they should put me into the dungeon" (vv. 14,15). These verses reveal the heart and thoughts of Joseph. They show how human he really was. But his trials were inhuman; they were extremely hard to bear.

There was nothing wrong with Joseph's seeking release, but he found that waiting for God's time is often one of the hardest things to do. Joseph was not rebuked by God for seeking his release because God knew the heartache Joseph had.

Regardless of what you are going through, God understands your deepest emotions; He knows how you feel. Hebrews 4:14-16 tells us, "Seeing then that we have a great high priest, that is passed into the heavens, Jesus the Son of

God, let us hold fast our profession. For we have not an high priest which cannot be touched with the feeling of our infirmities; but was in all points tempted like as we are, yet without sin. Let us therefore come boldly unto the throne of grace, that we may obtain mercy, and find grace to help in time of need." Compare these verses with Hebrews 2:18: "For in that he himself hath suffered being tempted, he is able to succour [help] them that are tempted." Many times I have gone to Psalm 103, for it has been such a blessing to my heart, especially verses 13,14: "Like as a father pitieth his children, so the Lord pitieth them that fear him. For he knoweth our frame; he remembereth that we are dust."

The fact that Joseph asked the butler to remember him showed his explicit faith that he had God's interpretation of the butler's dream. Joseph had confidence it was going to come to pass exactly as he had said.

The Baker's Dream

When the chief baker saw that the interpretation of the chief butler's dream was favorable, he shared his dream with Joseph also: "I had three white baskets on my head: and in the uppermost basket there was all manner of bakemeats for Pharaoh; and the birds did eat them out of the basket upon my head" (Gen. 40:16,17). Doubtlessly, the baker thought he would be restored to his position just as the butler was going to be, but Joseph's words to him were solemn ones: "This is the interpretation thereof: The three baskets are three days: Yet within three days shall Pharaoh lift up thy head from off thee, and shall hang thee on a tree; and the birds shall eat thy flesh from off thee" (vv. 18,19).

Joseph's faithfulness is seen even in his interpretation of the baker's dream. As sad as it was to deliver such a message, Joseph would not swerve from the truth for one moment, even for his own advantage. He realized that it was his responsibility to pass on what God had revealed to him.

Faithfulness is the characteristic that is so greatly needed in our lives today. The Word of God says, "It is required in stewards, that a man be found faithful" (I Cor. 4:2). This is the chief requirement of one to whom God delegates responsibility. The faithfulness of the Apostle Paul is seen from his words to the Ephesian elders: "I kept back nothing that was profitable unto you, but have shewed you, and have taught you publickly, and from house to house" (Acts 20:20). Paul went on to tell them that he was now going to Jerusalem although he did not know what would happen to him there. Although he expected the worst, he said, "But none of these things move me, neither count I my life dear unto myself, so that I might finish my course with joy, and the ministry, which I have received of the Lord Jesus, to testify the gospel of the grace of God" (v. 24). Paul was greatly used because he was faithful. Men are desperately needed today who will be faithful to God regardless of the cost.

From Joseph's words to the chief baker, it is evident that we are not to give people just half the truth. Joseph refused to be disloyal to God by withholding truth. As we study the Scriptures we see that God follows this principle. When telling us about the great men of faith, such as Abraham, Isaac and Jacob, God tells us of their failures as well as of their successes. As we speak to others, we should be kind and considerate, but we should never spare them from knowing the whole truth about the awfulness of sin and their need to be rightly related to Jesus Christ.

Time proved that Joseph had given God's interpretation of the dreams, for "it came to pass the third day, which was Pharaoh's birthday, that he made a feast unto all his servants: and he lifted up the head of the chief butler and of the chief baker among his servants. And he restored the chief butler unto his butlership again; and he gave the cup into Pharaoh's hand: but he hanged the chief baker: as Joseph had interpreted to them" (Gen. 40:20-22).

A Forgotten Man

As Joseph knew that the chief butler was now back in his position, no doubt the hope of getting out of prison grew brighter. Surely the butler would remember Joseph to Pharaoh as Joseph had asked. But whatever hopes Joseph had were dashed to pieces for the Scriptures say, "Yet did not the chief butler remember Joseph, but forgat him" (v. 23). Joseph had been concerned about the butler when he was sad and had tried to do all he could to encourage him, but now the butler forgot him completely. What ungratefulness.

Does the ungratefulness of people distress you? Perhaps you have done something for someone and have had to put forth much extra effort, but then they either take it for granted or soon forget it altogether. Does it bother you because you are not recognized for what you have done?

After the chief butler was released, Joseph spent two years in prison. How easy it would have been for him to have thought that God had forgotten him. But there is no indication that Joseph felt sorry for himself. He did not cry out for the justice of God to be executed, but he patiently waited to be released from prison in God's time. He was learning many spiritual lessons by the things he was suffering. This test of the soul was bringing Joseph to see that even his mind must be totally committed to God. All things were working together for Joseph's good and God's glory even though Joseph did not completely understand.

The Apostle Paul learned to trust God in the midst of difficult circumstances and was able to say, "Not that I speak in respect of want: for I have learned, in whatsoever state I am, therewith to be content" (Phil. 4:11). This is what we need to learn also.

Joseph's years of waiting in prison must have been terribly hard for him. What humiliation! Hate could have crept in so easily. But his soul was being tempered for his future responsibility and exaltation. God knew when that day would be, but Joseph did not. Nor did God reveal it to Joseph because that would have destroyed His process of discipline in bringing Joseph to an explicit faith and trust under every condition.

Joseph's test had a maturing and steadying effect upon his character. Daily faithfulness in ordinary duties is the best preparation for future service. In many respects, those years in prison were without doubt the most vital and critical years of Joseph's life. It had already been over 10 years since he had been sold as a slave, and it would have been very easy for him to have doubted the validity of the dreams God had given him. Just when there seemed to be hope of getting out of prison, the butler forgot about him.

Remember Moses? He spent 40 years on the backside of the desert while God was working with him—preparing him to be an effective instrument. How long does God have to work with us until we are ready to serve Him with unquestioned loyalty and obedience?

Three Things to Remember

If you are now going through testing, there are three things you should especially remember. First, God's way is the wisest way. Training is always accompanied by some type of hardship. Even athletes realize they cannot properly train without giving up some of the pleasures of life and enduring the hardship of training. God trains us through chastening, and Hebrews 12:11 says, "Now no chastening for the present seemeth to be joyous, but grievous: nevertheless afterward it yieldeth the peaceable fruit of righteousness unto them which are exercised thereby."

Second, God's time is the best time. God was working out His purpose through Joseph. It was impossible for Joseph to realize it at the time, but later he could look back and see that God's time had been exactly right—everything had worked out. But imagine the lonely years of waiting.

It is important that we learn this lesson. The Lord Jesus Christ Himself experienced it, and now He indwells us to teach us this lesson also. God does not act too early nor too late. He is never in a hurry but accomplishes things in His own time. Too many of us either lag behind or run ahead of God's time. But we need to remember that the clock of divine providence keeps strict time. Because of our circumstances it may appear to be slow at times and fast at others, but the all-wise God knows precisely when to act.

Third, God's grace is sufficient. He will give us the grace we need to be patient. James 1:4 says, "But let patience have her perfect work, that ye may be perfect and entire, wanting nothing." The word "perfect" means "mature" or "complete." God is seeking to teach us valuable lessons so we will be mature believers. Hebrews 10:36 tells us, "For ye have need of patience, that, after ye have done the will of God, ye might receive the promise." The secret of waiting *for* God is waiting *on* God. We do this through prayer, fellowship, faithful obedience, and complete trust in Him.

When God calls us to higher service, His summons may come in unexpected ways and at unexpected times. If we are not waiting on Him, we will not be ready and He will have to pass us by.

The Way of Spiritual Advancement

Joseph was advancing, but not according to human standards. Consider how God worked at every major turn of his life. Had Joseph been killed by his brothers instead of sold as a slave, there would have been no Egypt experience. Had he yielded to the temptation of Potiphar's wife, he would have missed the chief butler, whose dream he interpreted and who eventually was responsible for getting him out of prison. Or, had he been unbelieving and had he refused to interpret the dreams of the butler and baker, he would not have had the opportunity to interpret Pharaoh's dream because no one would have known about him.

Remember, in God's economy the way up is first down. We see this illustrated even in the life of the Lord Jesus Christ. The Apostle Paul told the believers at Philippi, "Let this mind be in you, which was also in Christ Jesus: who, being in the form of God, thought it not robbery to be equal with God: but made himself of no reputation, and took upon him the form of a servant, and was made in the likeness of men: and being found in fashion as a man, he humbled himself, and became obedient unto death, even the death of the cross. Wherefore God also hath highly exalted him, and given him a name which is above every name: that at the name of Jesus every knee should bow, of things in heaven, and things in earth, and things under the earth; and that every tongue should confess that Jesus Christ is Lord, to the glory of God the Father" (Phil. 2:5-11).

If we are to experience the way up with God, we must experience the way down as far as self is concerned. We must learn to be sustained in our suffering—not to faint but to endure—for "in due season we shall reap, if we faint not" (Gal. 6:9). So while we wait patiently for Him, let us rest in the Lord. If we do this, we will be able to say to the Lord as David's servants said to him, "Behold, thy servants are ready to do whatsoever my lord the king shall appoint" (II Sam. 15:15).

Out of Prison at Last

During his time in prison—even after he had interpreted the dreams of the butler and the baker—Joseph did not know when or if he would ever be released from prison. But his time came at last. Once again a dream played an important part in his life. God's Word says, "And it came to pass at the end of two full years, that Pharaoh dreamed: and, behold, he stood by the river. And, behold, there came up out of the river seven well favoured kine [cows] and fatfleshed; and they fed in a meadow. And, behold, seven other kine came up after them out of the river, ill favoured and leanfleshed; and stood by the other kine upon the brink of the river. And the ill favoured and leanfleshed kine did eat up the seven well favoured and fat kine. So Pharaoh awoke. And he slept and dreamed the second time: and, behold, seven ears of corn [grain] came up upon one stalk, rank and good. And, behold, seven thin ears and blasted with the east wind sprung up after them. And the seven thin ears devoured the seven rank and full ears. And Pharaoh awoke, and, behold, it was a dream. And it came to pass in the morning that his spirit was troubled; and he sent and called for all the magicians of Egypt, and all the wise men thereof: and Pharaoh told them his dream; but there was none that could interpret them unto Pharaoh" (Gen. 41:1-8).

When none was found to interpret Pharaoh's dream, finally the sluggish memory of the chief butler was stirred. He told Pharaoh, "I do remember my faults this day" (v. 9). The butler recounted how he and the baker had been put into prison and how Joseph had interpreted their dreams and that their dreams came to pass as he interpreted them.

Then "Pharaoh sent and called Joseph, and they brought him hastily out of the dungeon: and he shaved himself, and changed his raiment, and came in unto Pharaoh" (v. 14). The call was urgent. Joseph had time only to shave and dress properly to be presentable to the king. This was the moment that all the deepening adversity of the previous 13 years had been preparing him for. He had no time now to think or to design elaborate plans—he had time only to act.

What is in us comes out in a crisis. When there is no time for preparation and pretense, our true character is revealed. But the key to Joseph's life was obvious—he walked in the pure light of God's fellowship. He had learned the difference between the mind of the flesh and the mind of the Spirit.

Pharaoh told Joseph, "I have dreamed a dream, and there is none that can interpret it: and I have heard say of thee, that thou canst understand a dream to interpret it" (v. 15). Without a moment's hesitation Joseph said, "It is not in me: God shall give Pharaoh an answer of peace" (v. 16).

In essence he was saying, "I can't interpret your dream, but God can." Joseph had learned to have no confidence in the flesh but only confidence in God.

Joseph had passed the test of the soul which involved the mind, emotions and will. His years in the dungeon had brought him to see that even his mind must be completely committed to God and that God was God of the soul-life also.

Chapter 5

The Test of Prosperity and Advancement

Joseph could have viewed his trials in two different ways. The viewpoint he took made the significant difference in his spiritual life and in the peace he had in the midst of trial. There was the human side and the divine side. From the human side, Joseph's suffering in prison was due to injustice on the part of Potiphar and his wife, plus the ingratitude on the part of the king's butler. Although Joseph was innocent, he suffered.

But from the divine side, these years were permitted by God for the purpose of training and preparing Joseph for the great work that lay before him. Even though Joseph could not understand all the details at the time, God was working all things together for good to bring about His purpose through him.

When we look only at the human side of our trials, we will become discouraged. At the time of our tests, we may not see how the things involved could possibly work together for good, but our confidence needs to be in God. The Apostle Paul said with certainty, "We know that all things work together for good to them that love God. . . ." (Rom. 8:28). Certainly Paul was not able to understand the circumstances at all times, but his confidence was in God alone. If we walk only according to what we can see, we are not living by faith. We are to trust in God's love and grace and in His sovereign purpose for us. When we do this, we will have lasting peace in our hearts.

When things happen in your life that cannot be understood, turn to the Book of Philippians and read verses 6 and 7 of chapter 4: "Be careful for nothing; but in every thing by prayer and supplication with thanksgiving let your requests be made known unto God. And the peace of God, which passeth all understanding, shall keep your hearts and minds through Christ Jesus." To "be careful for nothing" means that we are not to be anxious about things. Let us bring *everything* to God by prayer and supplication, being sure not to forget the giving of thanks at the time of the prayer. This is faith.

There are several lessons we should learn from the life of Joseph in addition to those we have already pointed out. First, we are to put no confidence in man, for man at his best will only fail us. This was exemplified by the butler who, when he was released from prison, completely forgot about Joseph. Had Joseph totally depended on him, he would never have been able to understand why he still had to spend two years in prison. Never put your confidence in man.

The Prophet Jeremiah spoke the words of God when he said, "Thus saith the Lord; Cursed be the man that trusteth in man, and maketh flesh his arm, and whose heart departeth from the Lord. For he shall be like the heath in the desert, and shall not see when good cometh; but shall inhabit the parched places in the wilderness, in a salt land and not inhabited. Blessed is the man that trusteth in the Lord, and whose hope the Lord is. For he shall be as a tree planted by the waters, and that spreadeth out her roots by the river, and shall not see when heat cometh, but her leaf shall be green; and shall not be careful in the year of drought, neither shall cease from yielding fruit. The heart is deceitful above all things, and desperately wicked: who can know it? I the Lord search the heart, I try the reins, even to give every man according to his ways, and according to the fruit of his doings" (Jer. 17:5-10).

Second, we learn from Joseph's life that we need to turn from the failures of man to the faithfulness of God. We can always count on the fact that God is faithful. Isaiah 49:15,16 says, "Can a woman forget her sucking child, that she should not have compassion on the son of her womb? yea, they may forget, yet will I not forget thee. Behold, I have graven thee upon the palms of my hands; thy walls are continually before me." God will never forget us. He provides the help we need at exactly the right time. Like Mary and Martha, we sometimes think the Lord has waited too long. He waited two days while Lazarus died, but He came at just the right time to bring glory to His Father and to cause people to place their faith in Him. He told Martha, "Said I not unto thee, that, if thou wouldest believe, thou shouldest see the glory of God?" (John 11:40).

Third, we learn that we need to wait on the Lord. All your plans may seem to be shattered and every door may seem to be closed, but you will be greatly blessed as you wait on the Lord. In your trials you may cry out to the Lord wondering when the night of your difficulty will pass and the morning of blessing will appear, but God promises to bless those who wait on Him. The Word of God says, "They that wait upon the Lord shall renew their strength; they shall mount up with wings as eagles; they shall run, and not be weary; and they shall walk, and not faint" (Isa. 40:31).

There had been many things that had happened to Joseph, and some had seemed totally unrelated to others. But when Joseph was called to stand before Pharaoh, everything suddenly began to fit together. God is not an opportunist—He does not wait until the circumstances are right to take action. Rather, God in His sovereignty brings about the circumstances which produce the right time for Him to act. God had been carefully watching over and training His man for the task He had chosen for him and had caused him to dream about. Now, after 13 years of waiting amid great trials and many temptations, Joseph suddenly began to see why God had worked in such ways in his life. All along, Joseph had known that God was faithful, but now he began to see the expression of God's faithfulness, and he saw more links fit into the marvelous chain of events.

Pharaoh Rehearses Dreams

Pharaoh rehearsed his dream to Joseph. In his dream, Pharaoh had seen seven fat cows come up out of the river and feed in a meadow. Then he saw seven lean cows come up out of the river and stand by the others. The lean cows ate up the seven fat cows. Pharaoh awoke at this point, but when he went back to sleep he dreamed another dream. He saw seven ears of grain that came up on one stock, full and good. But then he saw seven thin ears that were blighted by the east wind. The seven thin ears devoured the seven fat ones. Then Pharaoh awoke. Pharaoh told Joseph that he had told his dreams to the magicians, but no one had been able to interpret them for him.

Pharaoh's dreams were used of God to perform His will concerning Joseph. It was no accident that Pharaoh dreamed as he did. Proverbs 21:1 says, "The king's heart is in the hand of the Lord, as the rivers of water: he turneth it whithersoever he will." God's time had come and His man, Joseph, was now ready.

We always need to remember that the most trivial as well as the most important thing can be used by God to accomplish His purpose. God is able to use the unlikely circumstance as well as the likely circumstance to develop His plan. We have seen how Satan used Potiphar's wife to test Joseph and how Satan also used the chief butler to test him. The former test was to put Joseph in prison; the latter test was to keep him in prison. But all of this was in vain for Satan, once God began to work. Then it was evident that God had been guiding the circumstances all along. When the proper time came, God brought forth the man of His purpose and set him in a place where he could directly carry out the will of God. It is always God's prerogative to use all things for the accomplishment of His grand and glorious purpose.

Colossians 1:16,17 tells us, "For it was in Him that all things were created, in heaven and on earth, things seen and things unseen, whether thrones, dominions, rulers or authorities; all things were created and exist through Him (by

His service, intervention) and in and for Him. And He Himself existed before all things and in Him all things consist—cohere, are held together" (Amp.). God is sovereign, and we can count on Him to carry out His purpose as He wills.

Failure of World's Wisdom

When the magicians of Egypt were called before Pharaoh to interpret his dreams, no one was able to interpret them. This reminds us of Christ's statement in Luke 10:21: "In that same hour He rejoiced and gloried in the Holy Spirit and said, I thank You, Father, Lord of heaven and earth, that You have concealed these things [relating to salvation] from the wise and understanding and learned, and revealed them to babes—the childish, unskilled and untaught. Yes, Father, for such was Your gracious will and choice and good pleasure" (Amp.). God hid the interpretation of the dreams from the wise men of Egypt, but He revealed it to Joseph, a babe in comparison.

The inability of the wise men to interpret Pharaoh's dreams, emphasizes the truth later recorded in I Corinthians 3:18,19: "Let no person deceive himself. If any one among you supposes that he is wise in this age—let him discard his [worldly] discernment and recognize himself as dull, stupid and foolish, without [true] learning and scholarship; let him become a fool that he may become [really] wise. For this world's wisdom is foolishness—absurdity and stupidity—with God. For it is written, He lays hold of the wise in their [own] craftiness" (Amp.).

Egypt was a symbol of the world. During the time of Joseph, Egypt was the center of learning and culture—it was a proud leader among ancient civilizations. But the people were idol worshipers; they did not know Jehovah. But now Pharaoh was made to see that all human resources and wisdom are powerless and worthless and that true wisdom comes only from God. How wonderful it would be if leaders in today's world would also come to that realization! "The secret of the Lord is with them that fear Him" (Ps. 25:14). If world leaders would turn to the Scriptures and seek God's face, they would learn what is shortly going to come to pass.

From the results of Joseph's time in prison, we see that patience had had her perfect work. God's man was now ready. All things had been working together for Joseph's good, although he had not always recognized it.

What a picture it was when Joseph was called before Pharaoh! It was the meeting of a mighty monarch and an unknown slave. Joseph had gone from the dungeon to the throne. His father had rebuked him for his dream, and his brothers had utterly rejected him and had sold him into slavery. But now Joseph found himself standing before the mighty monarch of the greatest nation on earth at that time.

Pharaoh said to Joseph, "I have dreamed a dream, and there is none that can interpret it: and I have heard say of thee, that thou canst understand a dream to interpret it" (Gen. 41:15). No doubt Pharaoh thought Joseph was another of the wise magicians, but Joseph's first words quickly dispelled any thoughts about his having secret powers. Joseph answered Pharaoh, "It is not in me: God shall give Pharaoh an answer of peace" (v. 16). This statement was more than a humble disclaimer—Joseph was giving direct credit to God.

By his words, "not in me," Joseph was utterly disregarding himself and his own fate. He was not devising a way for some glory to come to him so that he might be able to stay out of prison or better his life in any way. He had only one thought in mind—the glory of God. This was always the supreme and controlling thought in Joseph's life. In this sense, he was like the Lord Jesus Christ who said, "I have glorified thee on the earth: I have finished the work which thou gavest me to do" (John 17:4). Everything was done to the glory of God. The Apostle Paul stated his supreme desire in these words: "For to me to live is Christ, and to die is gain" (Phil. 1:21).

After Pharaoh told his dreams to Joseph, God revealed through Joseph that the dreams had to do with seven years of plenty, followed by seven years of great famine. Joseph told

Pharaoh, "This is the thing which I have spoken unto Pharaoh: What God is about to do he sheweth unto Pharaoh. Behold, there come seven years of great plenty throughout all the land of Egypt: and there shall arise after them seven years of famine; and all the plenty shall be forgotten in the land of Egypt; and the famine shall consume the land" (Gen. 41:28-30). Joseph explained to Pharaoh that actually there had not been two dreams but one, which doubly emphasized the same thing. Joseph said, "For that the dream was doubled unto Pharaoh twice; it is because the thing is established by God, and God will shortly bring it to pass" (v. 32).

Joseph's Advice

Joseph then advised Pharaoh that every precaution should be taken during the seven years of plenty so there would be food available during the seven years of famine. Joseph instructed, "Now therefore let Pharaoh look out a man discreet and wise, and set him over the land of Egypt. Let Pharaoh do this, and let him appoint officers over the land, and take up the fifth part of the land of Egypt in the seven plenteous years. And let them gather all the food of those good years that come, and lay up corn under the hand of Pharaoh, and let them keep food in the cities. And that food shall be for store to the land against the seven years of famine, which shall be in the land of Egypt; that the land perish not through the famine" (vv. 33-36). In all of this, Joseph did not say a word about himself nor speak in behalf of his own need. He had died to self; the previous 13 years had completely erased any desires for self. He had seen God working and that was his supreme desire.

We who know Jesus Christ as Saviour have also died to self. Note, it is not that we *should* die to self but that we *have* died to self. God's Word makes this truth very clear. Romans 6:6 says, "Knowing this, that our old man is [was] crucified with him, that the body of sin might be destroyed [rendered inoperative], that henceforth we should not serve sin." Our crucifixion took place when Christ died on the cross for us. It is not that we ought to die but that we have died. Our need now is to apply this truth, by faith, to ourselves. The Lord Jesus Christ said, "If any man will come after me, let him deny himself, and take up his cross daily, and follow me. For whosoever will save his life shall lose it: but whosoever will lose his life for my sake, the same shall save it" (Luke 9:23,24). Notice what the person is to deny—not things but himself. This involves saying No to selfish desires and saying Yes to Christ's desires. Through His death, He has broken the power of sin over us so that it is possible for us to say No to sin and Yes to Christ. Self is our greatest enemy; it will attempt to keep us from saying Yes to Christ.

Joseph's Character

There were many traits that were especially prominent at this time in Joseph's life. He had integrity—he was utterly sincere and honest. He had a closed code of values—he did not consider revising them. He was diligent—he stuck to the job at hand even though he could not see far in the future. There was nobility in his life—he had an excellence of character and a magnanimous nature. He had courage. He had humility. He was conscientious in all that he did.

Joseph had a well-rounded character. He was always ready, ever conscientious, never sacrificing his principles, faithful, and fearless before every crisis. No wonder that after Joseph finished his interpretation, Pharaoh said to his servants, "Can we find such a one as this is, a man in whom the Spirit of God is?" (Gen. 41:38). Here the king put his finger on the key to Joseph's life. Only a God-indwelt believer could have such a testimony as Joseph had.

Every believer during the present age is indwelt by God. The Apostle Paul said, "I am [was] crucified with Christ: nevertheless I live; yet not I, but Christ liveth in me: and the life which I now live in the flesh I live by the faith [faithfulness] of the Son of God, who loved me, and gave himself for me" (Gal. 2:20). Therefore, Paul could also say, "I can do all things through Christ which strengtheneth me" (Phil. 4:13).

Joseph did not need to advertise that he was indwelt by God—it was obvious even to an idol-worshiping king. If you are a Christian, do you realize that you are also indwelt by God? Do others know it, too, because of the difference they see in your life?

Words for Today

Every Christian ought to seriously consider the words of the following two passages of Scripture:

"Besides this you know what [a critical] hour this is, how it is high time now for you to wake up out of your sleep—rouse to reality. For salvation (final deliverance) is nearer to us now than when we first believed—adhered to, trusted in and relied on Christ, the Messiah. The night is far gone [and] the day is almost here. Let us then drop (fling away) the works and deeds of darkness and put on the [full] armor of light. Let us live and conduct ourselves honorably and becomingly as in the [open light of] day; not in reveling (carousing) and drunkenness, not in immorality and debauchery (sensuality and licentiousness), not in quarreling and jealousy. But clothe yourself with the Lord Jesus Christ, the Messiah, and make no provision for [indulging] the flesh—put a stop to thinking about the evil cravings of your physical nature—to [gratify its] desires (lusts)" (Rom. 13:11-14, Amp.).

"Take no part in and have no fellowship with the fruitless deeds and enterprises of darkness, but instead [let your lives be so in contrast as to] expose and reprove and convict them. For it is a shame even to speak of or mention the things that [such people] practice in secret. But when anything is exposed and reproved by the light, it is made visible and clear; and where everything is visible and clear there is light. Therefore He says, Awake, O sleeper, and arise from the dead, and Christ shall shine [make day dawn] upon you and give you light. Look carefully then how you walk! Live purposefully and worthily and accurately, not as the unwise and witless, but as wise—sensible, intelligent people; making the very most of the time—buying up each opportunity— because the days are evil. Therefore do not be vague and thoughtless and foolish, but understanding and firmly grasping what the will of the Lord is. And do not get drunk with wine, for that is debauchery; but ever be filled and stimulated with the (Holy) Spirit" (Eph. 5:11-18, Amp.).

Pharaoh's Response

Joseph now came to the greatest test of his life thus far—exaltation and prosperity. Pharaoh said to Joseph, "Forasmuch as God hath shewed thee all this, there is none so discreet and wise as thou art: thou shalt be over my house, and according unto thy word shall all my people be ruled: only in the throne will I be greater than thou. And Pharaoh said unto Joseph, See, I have set thee over all the land of Egypt. And Pharaoh took off his ring from his hand, and put it upon Joseph's hand, and arrayed him in vestures of fine linen, and put a gold chain about his neck; and he made him to ride in the second chariot which he had; and they cried before him, Bow the knee: and he made him ruler over all the land of Egypt. And Pharaoh said unto Joseph, I am Pharaoh, and without thee shall no man lift up his hand or foot in all the land of Egypt" (Gen. 41:39-44).

The hands that had known the hard toil of a slave were now adorned by the king's ring. Joseph's feet had been freed from the torment of the fetters, and now a gold chain was put around his neck. Joseph had lost his coat of many colors 13 years earlier when his brothers took it from him in anger and jealousy. Later, he had left his outer garment behind in the hands of Potiphar's wife when he had fled from her. But now he was given a royal wardrobe of fine linen. Once Joseph was treated as offscouring by the Egyptians, but now all Egypt was commanded to bow before him as he rode on the second chariot as the prime minister of Egypt.

All of this took place because Joseph sought to please God and resisted the temptation to sin. Rather than gratifying the flesh, Joseph sought to glorify God. Joseph found that godliness paid great dividends. He experienced the truth of the principle later stated in Matthew 6:33: "But seek ye first the kingdom of God, and his righteousness; and all these things shall be added unto you."

Dangers of Prosperity

The question now before Joseph was, Would he be able to accept prosperity and still keep his heart right with God? He was only 30 years old at this time and his new position and prosperity could have easily turned his attention away from spiritual things. However, God had been preparing him for 13 years—since Joseph had been sold as a slave by his brothers. These years of training were needed to prepare Joseph's character and to give him strength for the test he was now facing. Although Joseph's newfound prosperity provided an extreme test to see if he would keep his heart right with God, it has been a principle of God in every age that He never tests a man beyond what he is able to bear. Every believer is assured, "There hath no temptation taken you but such as is common to man: but God is faithful, who will not suffer [permit] you to be tempted above that ye are able; but will with the temptation also make a way to escape, that ye may be able to bear it" (I Cor. 10:13). God knew that Joseph was now ready for the severe test of prosperity because of all the lessons Joseph had learned in the previous 13 years.

Consider how prosperity can affect a person. Prosperity often brings pride, and "pride goeth before destruction" (Prov. 16:18). One has only to think of such men as Nebuchadnezzar and Herod to realize that this is true. The Word of God also makes clear that "only by pride cometh contention" (Prov. 13:10). The Bible also says, "God resisteth the proud, and giveth grace to the humble" (I Pet. 5:5).

Prosperity often makes a man hard and selfish. Frequently it causes him to forget the friends of his humble youth. And worst of all it often causes him to forget God.

Joseph possessed both intellectual and moral gifts. Such an advancement would have ruined a man of small character, but because of his moral integrity, Joseph's head was not turned. In the advice that Joseph gave Pharaoh about how to handle the problem of famine, it was apparent that Joseph also had the gift of management. Because Joseph had been faithful in his little responsibilities, he was now qualified for great responsibilities. Although Joseph was still a young man, he possessed maturity, poise and stability which could be imparted only to a man who had been severely tested in his faith. His moral and spiritual equilibrium remained undisturbed. The discipline of the many years of training had not been wasted.

Not only did Pharaoh give Joseph a great position for interpreting his dreams and for giving such sound advice, but he also "called Joseph's name Zaphnath-paaneah [revealer of secret things]; and he gave him to wife Asenath the daughter of Poti-pherah priest of On. And Joseph went out over all the land of Egypt" (Gen. 41:45). Pharaoh changed Joseph's name but he could not change Joseph's heart. Most likely, Pharaoh did not like Joseph's Hebrew name and background, and this is why he gave him an Egyptian name. But Joseph was not easily influenced. Egypt symbolized the world, and although Joseph was in Egypt, Egypt was not in him. His life was not divided between secular and sacred. He was not the kind of person who would have one kind of ethics in business and another kind in church or at home. All his life was dedicated to God at all times. That is why he was successful and always ready for what God had for him to do.

Joseph's Sons

As time passed, "unto Joseph were born two sons before the years of famine came, which Asenath the daughter of

Poti-pherah priest of On bare unto him. And Joseph called the name of the firstborn Manasseh [forgetting]: For God, said he, hath made me forget all my toil, and all my father's house" (vv. 50,51). This does not mean that God had caused Joseph to forget about his family, but He caused him to forget about the trials of the past as related to his family. This is exactly what happens when a person walks with the Lord. The blessings are so many he forgets about the trials.

Joseph named his second son "Ephraim," which means "fruitful." Joseph said, "For God hath caused me to be fruitful in the land of my affliction" (v. 52). Joseph had forgotten the trials and now saw only the fruit that God had brought about in his life.

So it will be with us when we really grasp the significance of the truths stated in Romans 8:28,29: "And we know that all things work together for good to them that love God, to them who are the called according to his purpose. For whom he did foreknow, he also did predestinate to be conformed to the image of his Son, that he might be the firstborn among many brethren." As we are conformed more and more to the image of Jesus Christ, we will be so thrilled with what God has accomplished in our lives that we will tend to forget the tests and sufferings that were used to cause us to be conformed to God's Son.

The Apostle Paul's testimony was, "Brethren, I count not myself to have apprehended: but this one thing I do, forgetting those things which are behind, and reaching forth unto those things which are before, I press toward the mark for the prize of the high calling of God in Christ Jesus" (Phil. 3:13,14). What was Paul referring to when he said he was forgetting those things that were behind? He was forgetting all the trials and tests, the stonings and shipwrecks because his attention was focused on God and how he might glorify Him. Paul did not dwell on the past; he fixed his eyes on God and looked to the future glory and reward with Him.

The Apostle Peter wrote: "Beloved, think it not strange concerning the fiery trial which is to try you, as though some strange thing happened unto you: but rejoice, inasmuch as ye are partakers of Christ's sufferings; that, when his glory shall be revealed, ye may be glad also with exceeding joy" (I Pet. 4:12,13). When we see Jesus face to face, it will be impossible to compare the glory of that moment with the sufferings we have endured. This is why Peter said, "But the God of all grace, who hath called us unto his eternal glory by Christ Jesus, after that ye have suffered a while, make you perfect, stablish, strengthen, settle you" (I Pet. 5:10).

Undiminished Loyalty to God

In his new position and prosperity, Joseph resisted and repelled the natural temptations of pride and arrogance with the same thoroughness as he had the temptation of passion. He was never drawn away from his utter loyalty to God. Regardless of where he was, he stayed true to God. Joseph had gone through severe testings to bring him to this moment. God could not bring Joseph forth until Joseph was completely ready for the next advancement in his life. However, He knew when there had been enough tests.

In the midst of Job's severe testing he said, "He [God] knoweth the way that I take: when he hath tried me, I shall come forth as gold" (Job 23:10). Referring to tests and suffering, the Apostle Peter said, "Wherein ye greatly rejoice, though now for a season, if need be, ye are in heaviness through manifold temptations, that the trial of your faith, being much more precious than of gold that perisheth, though it be tried with fire, might be found unto praise and honour and glory at the appearing of Jesus Christ" (I Pet. 1:6,7).

God was not through with Joseph once He brought him before Pharaoh. This step of exaltation and prosperity was but a part of a far greater plan. God's chosen family, Jacob and his children, would be in great need during the years of famine, and God was placing His man in Egypt to take care of them during that time. But this meant that God had to keep Joseph's heart right concerning his family in order to use him in His plan. The crucial question was, Will Joseph disown his family now that he has been given a great position and prosperity? It would have been a natural reaction for Joseph to have turned against his family for what they had done to him. Also, the Hebrews were an abomination to the Egyptians (Gen. 46:34) and Joseph might have turned against his own just to get along better with the Egyptians.

Lasting Lessons

In concluding our study of this portion of Joseph's life, we see seven truths that are prominent. First, God has a purpose for every life. That the Apostle Paul realized this is evident from his words, "None of these things move me, neither count I my life dear unto myself, so that I might finish my course with joy, and the ministry, which I have received of the Lord Jesus, to testify the gospel of the grace of God" (Acts 20:24). Even the Lord Jesus said to the Heavenly Father, "I have finished the work which thou gavest me to do" (John 17:4).

Second, a purpose for every life calls for discipline as a means of preparation. Trials and suffering are a part of God's school in training the believer for a special work. Joseph had 13 years of discipline under the hand of God that he might be ready at God's time. Moses spent 40 years in the desert getting ready for the job God had for him.

Third, the duty of life is faithfulness. Joseph held fast to his integrity in spite of the most trying circumstances. His confidence was in God and His faithfulness. Joseph's faithfulness to God was evidenced by his faithfulness to his earthly masters as well.

Fourth, God will perform to the end what He has begun. The New Testament makes this clear when it says, "Being confident of this very thing, that he which hath begun a good work in you will perform it until the day of Jesus Christ" (Phil. 1:6). As we have seen, Job realized this too: "When he hath tried me, I shall come forth as gold" (Job 23:10).

Fifth, God is glorified when others are faithfully served. No matter who Joseph's master was—his earthly father,

Potiphar, the jailer or Pharaoh—Joseph glorified God by serving others faithfully.

Sixth, God proves Himself to those who trust Him. By the time Joseph was elevated to a position second to Pharaoh, it had been many years since the dreams of his youth. And even now they were not completely fulfilled. He had committed his way to the Lord and had trusted completely in Him, and he had no reservations about God's ability to bring His will to pass. And God proved Himself righteous in fulfilling Joseph's dreams.

Seventh, God's wisdom is verified by the outcome of events. Although Joseph's years of trials had been a mystery to him, his present position made him realize that God had known what He was doing all along. Joseph had witnessed the sufficiency of God for every situation. He was now prepared for anything else God would want to do through him.

That Joseph knew God's sovereign will was being accomplished is evident from the words he spoke to his brothers much later: "But now do not be distressed and disheartened, or vexed and angry with yourselves because you sold me here, for God sent me ahead of you to preserve life. God sent me before you to preserve you a posterity and to continue a remnant on the earth, to save your lives by a great escape and save for you many survivors. So now it was not you who sent me here, but God; and He has made me a father to Pharaoh, and lord of all his house, and ruler over all the land of Egypt" (Gen. 45:5,7,8,Amp.).

Chapter 6

Joseph as Saviour

God's purpose for Joseph was coming to a climax. The plan of God involved much more than Joseph alone; however, God was especially grooming him for a very important task. Joseph was God's chosen vessel to bring Jacob's descendants into Egypt. He was prepared for this task through many tests, and when the time was right, God exalted him and placed him where he could fulfill the divine purpose.

God had promised to make of Jacob a great nation, but at this time Jacob's family numbered no more than 70 people. In the land of the hostile Canaanites, there was danger that Jacob's descendants would be annihilated, or that they and the Canaanites would become amalgamated. God's plan was to send them to Egypt in order to preserve them. Under the protection of the Egyptians they would not be annihilated, and because the Egyptians would have nothing to do with the Hebrews, they would not become amalgamated with them. Also, Jacob's descendants, who were a growing people, needed territory and supplies which they could not find in Canaan at that time.

Therefore, it was God's plan to take Jacob's descendants to Egypt, where they could have room for expansion and, at the same time, keep their uniqueness as the chosen people of God. There they were to learn the arts of civilization and industry, and under much affliction they would eventually be consolidated as a nation and be brought out of Egypt to return to the land of Canaan. In order for God to accomplish

His purpose, He needed His man in Egypt. Joseph was that man.

Many years later, God needed another man to lead the nation out of Egypt, and that man was Moses. Both of these men received their training in Egypt. Joseph received his training through suffering in Egypt, whereas Moses received his training in the house of Pharaoh, followed by 40 years in the desert. Both were men of God, chosen for specific tasks, but God used different methods to train them.

The time had come for God to begin the work of getting Jacob and his descendants down to Egypt. But this could not be done until there was a complete cleansing of heart on the part of Joseph's brothers. To accomplish this, their consciences had to be awakened, sin had to be confessed, repentance (a complete turnabout) was absolutely necessary, and a new life had to be evidenced. Joseph did not initiate this program; however, God worked mightily through him and used him to accomplish His will.

Joseph had learned explicit obedience through what he had suffered. He had learned to wait on God—especially to wait on God's timing in all the details of life. Had Joseph given in to his natural desires, he would no doubt have run ahead of God in the plan. Because of Joseph's love for his father and his brothers, particularly Benjamin, Joseph had to use great restraint to keep from running ahead of God. But an attempt to hurry God's program would have ruined it. Joseph was victorious in controlling his feelings and waiting on God.

Because of the sin they had committed against God and their father and Joseph, the brothers needed complete reconciliation. We see that on their first encounter with Joseph, God was bringing them to face this fact. There was to be no compromise in the reconciliation; it had to be thorough and complete. As we make a further study of all that God brought to bear on Joseph's brothers, you may ask, Why was God so hard on them? It was necessary in order for God to bring them to the place of complete reconciliation with Himself and Joseph. Just as it has to be in salvation, this had to be God's work, not man's.

God used circumstances to bring about the reconciliation. In this case, the particular circumstance He used was a famine. There had been seven years of plenty, just as Joseph's interpretation of Pharaoh's dream had predicted, but now the seven years of famine began. When the Egyptians needed food and cried out to Pharaoh, he told them, "Go unto Joseph; what he saith to you, do" (Gen. 41:55).

Egypt was not the only country affected by the famine. God's Word says that "the famine was over all the face of the earth: And Joseph opened all the storehouses, and sold unto the Egyptians; and the famine waxed sore in the land of Egypt. And all countries came into Egypt to Joseph for to buy corn [grain]; because that the famine was so sore in all lands" (vv. 56,57).

The land of Canaan was also experiencing famine. When Jacob learned that there was grain in the land of Egypt, he said to his sons, "Why do ye look one upon another? And he said, Behold, I have heard that there is corn [grain] in Egypt: get you down thither, and buy for us from thence; that we may live, and not die. And Joseph's ten brethren went down to buy corn [grain] in Egypt" (42:1-3). Joseph and his brothers were going to meet face to face! Joseph had successfully passed the tests God had brought to bear on him. He had passed the tests of adversity, of the body, of the soul (mind), and of prosperity. These tests were not related to his salvation, but they were used to bring him, as a believer, to the point where he was willing to place all his confidence in God. God brought Joseph to a place of reliance that could be described by the Apostle Paul's words centuries later: "I know whom I have believed, and am persuaded that he is able to keep that which I have committed unto him against that day" (II Tim. 1:12). Joseph also could have said, as did Paul, "Wherein I suffer trouble, as an evil doer, even unto bonds; but the word of God is not bound. Therefore I endure all things for the elect's sakes, that they may also obtain the salvation which is in Christ Jesus with eternal glory" (II Tim. 2:9,10).

The Test of the Inner Man

Having passed the other tests successfully, Joseph now faced the test of the inner man. He was now prosperous and powerful. In naming his first son "Manasseh," he expressed how God had enabled him to forget his toil and his father's house (Gen. 41:51). Would he now be willing to recognize and forgive his brethren—plus be used to fulfill God's program for them—after all the evil they had done to him? What was to be found in his spirit? Would it be vengeance or forgiveness?

Joseph now had an opportunity for retaliation. This is what made the test of the inner man such a severe test. His brothers had treated him hatefully and now that Joseph was the prime minister of the most powerful country in the world, there was danger that he would be proud and unforgiving.

The Scriptures say, "And Joseph's ten brethren went down to buy corn [grain] in Egypt. But Benjamin, Joseph's brother, Jacob sent not with his brethren; for he said, Lest peradventure mischief befall him. And the sons of Israel came to buy corn [grain] among those that came: for the famine was in the land of Canaan. And Joseph was the governor over the land, and he it was that sold to all the people of the land: and Joseph's brethren came, and bowed down themselves before him with their faces to the earth. And Joseph saw his brethren, and he knew them, but made himself strange unto them, and spake roughly unto them; and he said unto them, Whence come ye? And they said, From the land of Canaan to buy food. And Joseph knew his brethren, but they knew not him. And Joseph remembered the dreams which he dreamed of them, and said unto them, Ye are spies; to see the nakedness of the land ye are come" (Gen. 42:3-9).

God had instilled a carefully laid plan for Joseph to follow. The brothers were to be brought to repentance. Even the incident concerning Benjamin, which we shall be examining later, was to bring about a right heart attitude in them. Joseph was speaking through an interpreter; thus, he could withhold his identity from his brothers and was able to ascertain their hearts' true attitude.

Joseph was not acting in his own behalf; he was God's representative, used to bring about the fulfillment of God's plan. By delaying immediate identification, Joseph allowed God to work out this carefully laid plan. This was a great test for Joseph because he had to be willing to experience agony of heart for a couple more years before he dared to identify himself to his brothers. Had Joseph revealed his identity to his brothers at this time, even for the purpose of rebuking them for their sin, he would have done great harm to God's plan. This was painful waiting, but Joseph determined that God would be first in his life.

There was no vengeance in Joseph's heart. When his brothers bowed down and made obeisance to him, Joseph remembered his dreams. Yet, he did not take delight in his brothers' making obeisance to him but in God's being faithful in every detail. By now, Joseph saw that God's plan was being fulfilled through the circumstances that had occurred. Now he saw, as through God's eyes, that all the years of suffering and exile were the working out of the plan of transcendent wisdom.

God's plan went back long before Joseph's time. It began with Abraham when God promised to make a great nation of him (Gen. 12:1-3). This promise was confirmed to Isaac and later to Jacob. But Jacob and his descendants were not becoming a great nation in Canaan. Therefore, God's plan was to send them to Egypt, and Joseph was the crucial person God used to prepare their way. Joseph must have rejoiced to realize that he was such an important part in God's eternal plan. How greatly it must have humbled Joseph to realize that God was using him so mightily. It was the Holy Spirit indwelling Joseph that enabled him to love his brothers who were his enemies, to be their present saviour, and to lead them to repentance and then into the land of Egypt according to God's purpose.

Are you thrilled that, as believers, we have been united to Christ for the fulfilling of God's eternal purpose through His Church? Are you thrilled with the way God is working out His eternal purpose through you as an individual? Just as Joseph had to become the saviour of his brothers, we are the ones through whom Jesus really becomes the Saviour of the world. This is why He leaves us here after we receive Him as Saviour—to tell others about Him.

Each of us must someday give account to Jesus Christ for what we have done in His behalf. Writing by inspiration, the Apostle Paul said, "For we must all appear before the judgment seat of Christ; that every one may receive the things done in his body, according to that he hath done, whether it be good or bad" (II Cor. 5:10). In this same chapter, the Apostle Paul went on to say, "For the love of Christ constraineth us; because we thus judge, that if one died for all, then were all dead: and that he died for all, that they which live should not henceforth live unto themselves, but unto him which died for them, and rose again" (vv. 14,15).

Paul then set forth the believer's responsibility when he said, "And all things are of God, who hath reconciled us to himself by Jesus Christ, and hath given to us the ministry of reconciliation; to wit, that God was in Christ, reconciling the world unto himself, not imputing their trespasses unto them; and hath committed unto us the word of reconciliation. Now then we are ambassadors for Christ, as though God did beseech you by us: we pray you in Christ's stead, be ye reconciled to God" (vv. 18-20). In Christ, God has made reconciliation possible for everyone, and our responsibility is to take this message to them.

Had Joseph allowed his luxurious surroundings to cause him to think only of himself, God's plan would have failed. How much are we contributing to the failure of God's plan for the present age because we are thinking only of ourselves?

Let us be sure that we are doing what God has left us here to do.

Awakening the Conscience

More than 20 years had passed since Joseph's brothers had sold him into slavery. Perhaps they never mentioned to each other their violent acts against Joseph, although individually they may have thought about him as they remembered his agony of soul. Even though they might have refused to think about it during their waking hours, perhaps when sleeping they dreamed about the awful things they had done to their brother.

Their consciences had become dulled to sin. But the time had now come when God wanted to use Jacob's sons to found a nation. In order to fit them for their high destiny, God had to bring them into a right relationship with Himself. They had to be right with God and with others. But how could they be right if there was no repentance for the evil they had committed against Joseph. Perhaps you say, How can they be blamed when it all seemed to be a part of the plan of God? We should never submit to the Devil even though God can overrule and bring glory to Himself. Although things were turning out all right because God had overruled, the brothers needed to confess their sin in order to be right with God. The problem was how to get repentance from those with darkened hearts and dulled consciences.

Famine

But God is never at a loss. He is able to cause circumstances that will achieve His purpose. God brought pressure to bear on Joseph's brothers. The first step God used to awaken their consciences was to bring about famine in the land. A short time before, the brothers had had plenty and had been content. They had been unconcerned about what had happened to Joseph and the sins they had committed. But when the famine came, these men's hearts were opened at least to the extent that God could begin to work on their

consciences to bring about conviction. Their carnal security
was suddenly shattered.

Joseph's brothers were about to pass through a spiritual
exercise of which they were very much unaware. This is the
way God frequently deals with us. He may take things away
from us—material possessions or even loved ones—so that we
will begin to listen to Him and His Word. He uses this to
cause us to search out and confess the things in our hearts
that are wrong. The psalmist said, "Before I was afflicted I
went astray: but now have I kept thy word" (Ps. 119:67).

When Jacob learned that there was grain in Egypt, he
commissioned his sons to go there to buy some. While they
were thinking about Egypt, the sons must have been looking
at one another, because Jacob asked, "Why do ye look one
upon another?" (Gen. 42:1). Perhaps talk about Egypt
pierced their sleeping consciences. Is it possible that Jacob
had guessed what had gone on before? Whatever the case,
God used the famine to eventually bring Joseph's brothers to
the place of admitting their need.

God brought another pressure to bear on the brothers.
The Bible says that "Joseph's ten brethren went down to buy
corn [grain] in Egypt. But Benjamin, Joseph's brother, Jacob
sent not with his brethren; for he said, Lest peradventure
mischief befall him" (vv. 3,4). Why did Jacob refuse to let
the brothers take Benjamin with them? No doubt Jacob was
especially concerned about Benjamin since he was the
youngest, but it is also likely that Jacob no longer trusted his
older sons. Perhaps Jacob now suspected that they were
partly responsible for whatever had happened to Joseph. The
fact that Jacob refused to let the older brothers take
Benjamin along certainly indicated he did not have
confidence they would sufficiently take care of Benjamin.
God used this as another barb to prick their consciences.

Rough Treatment

The second step God used in awakening the consciences
of Joseph's brothers was to have Joseph treat them roughly.

When they bowed down before him, "Joseph saw his brethren, and he knew them, but made himself strange unto them, and spake roughly unto them; and he said unto them, Whence come ye? And they said, From the land of Canaan to buy food. And Joseph knew his brethren, but they knew not him. And Joseph remembered the dreams which he dreamed of them, and said unto them, Ye are spies; to see the nakedness of the land ye are come" (vv. 7-9). No doubt Joseph had been waiting for his brothers to come for food. Since the famine "was over all the face of the earth" (41:56), it was a certainty that they would eventually come to Egypt.

Although Joseph recognized his brothers, they did not recognize him. When they had last seen him, he was only 17 years old; now he was nearly 40. Also, at this time Joseph would have been arrayed with Egyptian garments and ornaments of rank. The brothers would never have guessed that the one they had sold into slavery was now the governor of Egypt. Perhaps they thought they might see their brother among the slaves as they walked along the roads in Egypt. Imagine them as they watched the slaves at work, wondering if one of them might be their own brother. But they were not looking for him in the place of royalty so they had no idea that the one standing before them now was Joseph.

Joseph's heart was bursting with the desire to disclose himself to his brothers, but he realized he dare not do this and spoil God's program. He had suffered too much to be disobedient now, even for love's sake. Joseph realized that God's plan was to bring his brothers to the place where they would have a new heart attitude as expressed by complete repentance. Joseph looked on his brothers with compassion and saw them as ones needing to be made right with God.

When you see those who are without Jesus Christ, is your heart moved with compassion? When you are in a crowd of people and realize that maybe 98 percent of them are not born again, how does it affect you? Does it mean anything to you, or are they just people?

Imprisonment

Joseph accused his brothers of being spies. Think of the contrast! Over 20 years ago they had accused Joseph of spying on them and telling their father on them; now he was accusing them of being spies. When they accused Joseph, they cast him into a pit. Now that he accused them, "he put them all together into ward three days" (42:17). Joseph's actions paralleled their actions many years before, but he did not do it for revenge.

Memory is one of the most marvelous faculties of our nature. Often when a person receives the kind of evil treatment that he has dealt to others, he remembers his sin and is convicted. The third step God used in awakening the consciences of Joseph's brothers was having them imprisoned. There God could bring even stronger conviction. Their guilt was beginning to strike home.

When Joseph accused his brothers of being spies, "they said unto him, Nay, my lord, but to buy food are thy servants come. We are all one man's sons; we are true men, thy servants are no spies. And he said unto them, Nay, but to see the nakedness of the land ye are come. And they said, Thy servants are twelve brethren, the sons of one man in the land of Canaan; and, behold, the youngest is this day with our father, and one is not. And Joseph said unto them, That is it that I spake unto you, saying, Ye are spies: hereby ye shall be proved: By the life of Pharaoh ye shall not go forth hence, except your youngest brother come hither. Send one of you, and let him fetch your brother, and ye shall be kept in prison, that your words may be proved, whether there be any truth in you: or else by the life of Pharaoh surely ye are spies" (vv. 10-16).

The brothers explained that their youngest brother was with their father and "one is not" (v. 13). Joseph's heart must have quickened when he heard this, for he knew they were referring to him with the words "one is not." How easy it would have been for him to have said something to give himself away. However, he restrained himself and took another course of action.

Another pressure that God brought to bear on the brothers was giving them time to think and to listen to the Spirit of God. There can be no conviction until the Spirit of God begins to work. Joseph acted in God's behalf when "he put them all together into ward three days" (v. 17).

Without the work of the Holy Spirit there is only remorse, not true conviction of guilt. In promising to send the Holy Spirit, the Lord Jesus Christ described His work: "And when he is come, he will reprove the world of sin, and of righteousness, and of judgment" (John 16:8). Too many times we ministers and evangelists are so anxious to have conviction brought to hearts that we try to bring it ourselves through deathbed stories or other means. However, true conviction comes only through the ministry of the Holy Spirit. He can use what we say to bring conviction, but we must realize that nothing we say will bring conviction if the Holy Spirit does not work. It is only when the Holy Spirit works that men will cry out, as did Isaiah, "Woe is me! for I am undone" (Isa. 6:5).

In prison, Joseph's brothers had time to think and to talk about why their situation was so desperate. On the third day Joseph said to them, "This do, and live; for I fear God: If ye be true men, let one of your brethren be bound in the house of your prison: go ye, carry corn for the famine of your houses: But bring your youngest brother unto me; so shall your words be verified, and ye shall not die. And they did so. And they said one to another, We are verily guilty concerning our brother, in that we saw the anguish of his soul, when he besought us, and we would not hear; therefore is this distress come upon us. And Reuben answered them, saying, Spake I not unto you, saying, Do not sin against the child; and ye would not hear? therefore, behold, also his blood is required. And they knew not that Joseph understood them; for he spake unto them by an interpreter" (Gen. 42:18-23).

Their consciences were now awake! They admitted their guilt in refusing to spare Joseph when they saw the anguish of his soul. They were totally unaware that Joseph understood them as they admitted their guilt.

Joseph's Response

All of this was too much for Joseph, and "he turned himself about from them, and wept" (v. 24). His heart was still tender toward them in spite of what they had done to him. Controlling himself, he "returned to them again, and communed with them, and took from them Simeon, and bound him before their eyes" (v. 24). It is possible that Simeon had been the leader in what the brothers had done to Joseph earlier, but now all the brothers were beginning to show true repentance. Verse 21 shows three aspects of this repentance: conscience—"we are verily guilty"; memory—"we saw the anguish of his soul"; and reason—"therefore is this distress come upon us." The brothers were being brought to an end of themselves.

Joseph responded in two ways, although his brothers noticed only one of his responses. First, he wept with a broken heart because of his love for his brothers—especially Benjamin—and for his father. Second, he bound Simeon in their presence. The brothers saw only the hardness which Joseph expressed; they did not know how tender his heart was underneath it all. Joseph's next actions brought even further conviction to them.

"Then Joseph commanded to fill their sacks with corn [grain], and to restore every man's money into his sack, and to give them provision for the way: and thus did he unto them. And they laded their asses with the corn [grain], and departed thence. And as one of them opened his sack to give his ass provender [fodder] in the inn, he espied his money; for, behold, it was in his sack's mouth. And he said unto his brethren, My money is restored; and, lo, it is even in my sack: and their heart failed them, and they were afraid, saying one to another, What is this that God hath done unto us?" (vv. 25-28).

A guilty conscience was very evident in the brothers now, and they misinterpreted the kindest gifts and deeds of mercy as something very, very hard. Their guilt made cowards of them. Their immediate reaction was, "What is this that God hath done unto us?" They were extremely sensitive about what they had done to Joseph, so now they interpreted every act as being a punishment for that sin. They accused God.

Has this also happened to you? Perhaps you wronged a dear friend and later felt guilty about it, but you did not make things right with him or God. Then, whenever the friend tried to express an act of kindness, you misinterpreted it as an act of retaliation. You were under such conviction that you overreacted. Of course, your dearest Friend is the Lord Jesus Christ Himself. Does it bother you when you do things that are not pleasing to Him? Is your conscience dulled—do you go right on as if nothing has happened? He has freely offered you the greatest of all gifts—Himself—but when you dishonor Him, you trample Him underfoot. You treat Him despitefully and crucify Him afresh when you go your selfish way rather than seeking to please Him. One of the best ways we please Him is by obeying His command to witness, as recorded in Matthew 28:18-20 and Acts 1:8.

God's first objective concerning Joseph's brothers had been accomplished—their consciences had been awakened. At this point, repentance seemed not to be very far off, thus making way for true forgiveness. As Joseph's tenderness of heart indicated when he stood before his brothers, he had forgiven them long ago—even though they did not realize it.

Back Home

When the brothers returned to Canaan, they rehearsed to their father all that had taken place in Egypt. They told how "the lord of the land" (Gen. 42:30) had spoken roughly to them, had kept Simeon in Egypt, and had demanded that they bring their youngest brother with them next time. Then the Scriptures say, "And it came to pass as they emptied their sacks, that, behold, every man's bundle of money was in his sack: and when both they and their father saw the bundles of money, they were afraid" (v. 35).

Realizing the trouble they were in, Jacob said to his sons, "Me have ye bereaved of my children: Joseph is not, and

Simeon is not, and ye will take Benjamin away: all these
things are against me" (v. 36). Jacob expressed a gross lack of
faith. He failed to see the timeless principle of God that "all
things work together for good to them that love God, to
them who are the called according to his purpose" (Rom.
8:28). All he could see was the immediate circumstances and,
as far as he was concerned, there was no hope whatever. The
son passed the tests better than the father. Joseph responded
to hopeless situations better than Jacob. Faith had conquered
for Joseph, but Jacob was slow to see that God could bring
good out of these circumstances.

Reuben tried to assure his father that Benjamin would be
safe when they took him to Egypt. Reuben said, "Slay my
two sons, if I bring him not to thee: deliver him into my
hand, and I will bring him to thee again" (Gen. 42:37). But it
was impossible for Jacob to see any possibility of allowing
Benjamin to go to Egypt. Jacob answered, "My son shall not
go down with you; for his brother is dead, and he is left
alone: if mischief befall him by the way in the which ye go,
then shall ye bring down my gray hairs with sorrow to the
grave" (v. 38).

Jacob did not think he could stand any more grief, but
his sons knew it was hopeless to return to Egypt without
their youngest brother. Although they didn't know it, they
were about to face other great tests.

Chapter 7

Reconciliation

When Jacob's sons returned from their first journey to Egypt and reported that it was necessary to take Benjamin the next time if they were to get food, Jacob utterly refused to let Benjamin go. However, the famine continued to be very severe and they were again in need of going to Egypt for grain. The Bible says, "And the famine was sore in the land. And it came to pass, when they had eaten up the corn [grain] which they had brought out of Egypt, their father said unto them, Go again, buy us a little food. And Judah spake unto him, saying, The man did solemnly protest unto us, saying, Ye shall not see my face, except your brother be with you" (Gen. 43:1-3).

Jacob commissioned his sons to go to Egypt again because they needed grain, but his sons knew there was no use in going if they did not take Benjamin with them. Judah told his father, "If thou wilt send our brother with us, we will go down and buy thee food: but if thou wilt not send him, we will not go down: for the man said unto us, Ye shall not see my face, except your brother be with you" (vv. 4,5). Jacob and his family were in danger of starving, but he did not want to risk losing Benjamin as he had lost Joseph. Jacob's sons were being put under a great test. They were put under this test to see if they had genuinely repented of their sin against Joseph and if they would show the evidence of a new life.

Jacob was greatly disappointed that his sons had admitted down in Egypt that they had another brother. They argued that they had no alternative. Finally, Judah lit upon a plan. He said to Jacob, "Send the lad with me, and we will arise and go; that we may live, and not die, both we, and thou, and also our little ones. I will be surety for him; of my hand shalt thou require him: if I bring him not unto thee, and set him before thee, then let me bear the blame for ever: for except we had lingered, surely now we had returned this second time" (vv. 8-10). Of course, it was little comfort to Jacob that Judah was willing to bear the blame if anything happened to Benjamin—that would not bring Benjamin back. But with no alternative because of their desperate circumstances, Jacob said, "If it must be so now, do this; take of the best fruits in the land in your vessels, and carry down the man a present, a little balm, and a little honey, spices, and myrrh, nuts, and almonds: and take double money in your hand; and the money that was brought again in the mouth of your sacks, carry it again in your hand; peradventure it was an oversight: take also your brother, and arise, go again unto the man: and God Almighty give you mercy before the man, that he may send away your other brother, and Benjamin. If I be bereaved of my children, I am bereaved" (vv. 11-14).

A Feast With Joseph

Jacob reluctantly let his sons take Benjamin to Egypt, and he gave them instructions as to what they should take along so they might be well received. The sons did as Jacob instructed. They "took that present, and they took double money in their hand, and Benjamin; and rose up, and went down to Egypt, and stood before Joseph" (v. 15). When Joseph saw his brothers—and Benjamin with them—he commanded the ruler of his house, "Bring these men home, and slay, and make ready; for these men shall dine with me at noon" (v. 16). Then conscience did its work again. The brothers had such guilt concerning Joseph that anything caused them to greatly fear—especially in the strange land of Egypt.

The ruler of Joseph's house "did as Joseph bade; and the man brought the men into Joseph's house. And the men were afraid, because they were brought into Joseph's house; and they said, Because of the money that was returned in our sacks at the first time are we brought in; that he may seek occasion against us, and fall upon us, and take us for bondmen, and our asses" (vv. 17,18).

The brothers had been so brave before when they sold Joseph into slavery, but now even hospitality brought fear to them. When a person is guilty of sin, almost everything brings fear to him.

The brothers talked to the steward of Joseph's house and explained how that on their previous trip they had found their money in their sacks and that now they had returned it and had brought other money to buy food. They emphasized to the steward that they had not stolen the money, but they admitted, "We cannot tell who put our money in our sacks" (v. 22). The steward replied, "Peace be to you, fear not: your God, and the God of your father, hath given you treasure in your sacks: I had your money. And he brought Simeon out unto them" (v. 23).

When Joseph arrived, he asked concerning their father, "Is your father well, the old man of whom ye spake? Is he yet alive?" (v. 27). His brothers assured him that their father was alive and in good health. When Joseph saw Benjamin, he asked, "Is this your younger brother, of whom ye spake unto me? And he said, God be gracious unto thee, my son" (v. 29).

Joseph was unable to restrain himself, and he "made haste; for his bowels [heart] did yearn upon his brother: and he sought where to weep; and he entered into his chamber, and wept there" (v. 30). What a moving account of the love of Joseph for Benjamin! Finally gaining control of himself, Joseph "washed his face, and went out, and refrained [controlled] himself, and said, Set on bread" (v. 31). Joseph still did not identify himself to his brothers. God's program was not yet completed. Joseph was well trained to wait for

God's time, regardless of how difficult it was because of his own emotions.

It is highly significant to observe the way they were seated at the meal. "They set on for him [Joseph] by himself, and for them by themselves, and for the Egyptians, which did eat with him, by themselves: because the Egyptians might not eat bread with the Hebrews; for that is an abomination unto the Egyptians" (v. 32). Not only were the brothers separated from the Egyptians and Joseph, but Joseph also had a separate seating arrangement for them. "They sat before him, the firstborn according to his birthright, and the youngest according to his youth: and the men marvelled one at another" (v. 33). Most likely, the reason they marveled was that they were astonished that this Egyptian ruler knew their ages and was able to seat them in the right order. This especially would bring fear to the brothers, for they would wonder what else he knew about them.

The brothers were then subjected to another test. When the food was served, Joseph "took and sent messes unto them from before him: but Benjamin's mess was five times so much as any of their's. And they drank, and were merry with him" (v. 34). The brothers were being tested regarding their attitude toward their younger brother. They had been envious of Joseph because of their father's special love for him. They might well have felt the same way toward Benjamin, because their father also had a special love for him. What would their reaction be to Benjamin's getting more attention than they at the banquet? Joseph was testing them and, at the same time, bestowing his love on Benjamin.

The Silver Cup

Then the brothers were put to another test. Joseph "commanded the steward of his house, saying, Fill the men's sacks with food, as much as they can carry, and put every man's money in his sack's mouth. And put my cup, the silver cup, in the sack's mouth of the youngest, and his corn [grain] money. And he did according to the word that Joseph had spoken" (44:1,2). The next morning the men were sent away at daybreak. They were not very far away when Joseph said to his steward, "Up, follow after the men; and when thou dost overtake them, say unto them, Wherefore have ye rewarded evil for good? Is not this it in which my lord drinketh, and whereby indeed he divineth? ye have done evil in so doing" (vv. 4,5).

Perhaps you say this was cruel. Maybe it seems cruel, but sometimes God has to do severe things to get people to see their sinfulness. Joseph's brothers were being severely tested to see what their reaction would be toward Benjamin when it was discovered that the silver cup was in his sack. Would they sacrifice him for their own safety as they once had done to Joseph?

The brothers, of course, disclaimed any knowledge of the silver cup, and they declared, "With whomsoever of thy servants it be found, both let him die, and we also will be my lord's bondmen" (v. 9). Joseph's steward replied, "Now also let it be according unto your words: he with whom it is found shall be my servant; and ye shall be blameless" (v. 10).

The sacks were speedily taken down and the search was begun. The steward "began at the eldest, and left at the youngest: and the cup was found in Benjamin's sack" (v. 12). The brothers were horrified! "They rent [tore] their clothes, and laded every man his ass, and returned to the city" (v. 13). They were now completely under the domination of Joseph. There was nothing they could do.

When they were brought in before Joseph, he said to them, "What deed is this that ye have done? wot [know] ye not that such a man as I can certainly divine?" (v. 15). Earlier, the brothers had said, "We shall see what will become of his dreams" (37:20). Now they were completely at the mercy of Joseph because his dreams had been fulfilled, even though they did not realize it was Joseph before whom they stood.

The Brothers' Defense

In defense, Judah said, "What shall we say unto my lord? what shall we speak? or how shall we clear ourselves? God hath found out the iniquity of thy servants: behold, we are my lord's servants, both we, and he also with whom the cup is found" (v. 16). The brothers had nowhere to turn; they could only cast themselves upon Joseph's mercy.

Judah admitted, "God hath found out the iniquity of thy servants." It is a timeless principle that God always finds out our iniquity. The Bible warns, "Be sure your sin will find you out" (Num. 32:23). All judgment for sin is not experienced in this life. Those who have rejected Jesus Christ as Saviour will stand before the Great White Throne Judgment, where they will be judged and cast into the lake of fire (Rev. 20:11-15). This is a certain judgment, even as Hebrews 9:27 tells us: "And as it is appointed unto men once to die, but after this the judgment." The unsaved will have no basis on which to stand when they appear before the judgment. Psalm 1:5 says, "Therefore, the ungodly shall not stand in the judgment, nor sinners in the congregation of the righteous." When the wrath of God is poured out, the words of Revelation 6:17 will be fulfilled: "For the great day of his wrath is come; and who shall be able to stand?"

Joseph's brothers had passed their final test. When Judah said that all of them, even Benjamin, would become servants, Joseph said, "God forbid that I should do so: but the man in whose hand the cup is found, he shall be my servant; and as for you, get you up in peace unto your father" (Gen. 44:17).

What follows is one of the greatest pieces of literature on human intercession. The spokesman was Judah. Reuben was the oldest and he usually spoke up, but he almost always spoke in self-justification. His mouth was now sealed. Neither did Simeon have anything to say. Possibly he had been the ringleader in the crime against Joseph, so what could he say now that would be of help? Benjamin was blameless, yet he was the one being accused and pronounced guilty. There was nothing he could say. Judah stood forth as the spokesman. It

was Judah who more than 20 years ago had stood at the
mouth of the pit and said to his brothers, "What profit is it if
we slay our brother, and conceal his blood? Come, and let us
sell him to the Ishmeelites, and let not our hand be upon
him; for he is our brother and our flesh" (37:26,27). But
Judah showed himself to be a different man as he now stood
before Joseph. There was nothing he could say to justify
himself or his brothers; he threw himself helplessly on
Joseph's mercy. His intercession revealed his changed
character as well as the changed character of his brothers.
Notice the gripping words of his intercession:

"O my lord, let your servant, I pray you, speak a word to
you in private, and let not your anger blaze against your
servant, for you are as Pharaoh [so I will speak as if directly
to him]. My lord asked his servants, saying, Have you a
father, or a brother? And we said to my lord, We have a
father, an old man, and a young [brother the] child of his
old age; and his brother is dead, and he alone is left of his
mother's [offspring], and his father loves him. And you said
to your servants, Bring him down to me, that I may set my
eyes on him. And we said to my lord, The lad cannot leave
his father; for if he should do so, his father would die. And
you told your servants, Unless your youngest brother comes
with you, you shall not see my face again.

"And when we went back to your servant my father, we
told him what my lord had said. And our father said, Go
again, and buy us a little food. But we said, We cannot go
down. If our younger brother is with us, then we will go
down; for we may not see the man's face, except our
youngest brother is with us. And your servant my father said
to us, You know that [Rachel] my wife bore me two sons:
and the one went out from me, and I said, Surely he is torn
to pieces, and I have never seen him since. And if you take
this son also from me, and harm or accident should befall
him, you will bring down my gray hairs with sorrow and evil
to Sheol.

"Now therefore when I come to your servant my father,
and the lad is not with us, when his life is bound up in the

lad's life, and his soul knit with the lad's soul, when he sees that the lad is not with us, he will die; and your servants will be responsible for his death and will bring down the gray hairs of your servant our father with sorrow to Sheol (the place of the dead). For your servant became security for the lad to my father, saying, If I do not bring him to you, then I will bear the blame to my father forever. Now therefore, I pray you, let your servant remain instead of the youth [to be] a slave to my lord; and let the young man go home with his [half] brothers. For how can I go up to my father if the lad is not with me? Lest I witness the woe and the evil that will come upon my father" (44:18-34, Amp.).

Judah's speech revealed that he had experienced a complete change of life and that his brothers had also.

The Power of Fear

Throughout God's dealings with Joseph's brothers, we see the moral power of fear. They were impressed and actuated by fear from first to last. It was fear that finally brought them to the place of true repentance, genuine conversion—a genuine change of heart.

It was when they were considering taking their first journey to Egypt that fear struck home to their hearts at the mention of that country. Then when they stood before Joseph the first time, they saw his apparent hardness and were again moved with fear. They were also filled with fear when they found their money in their sacks after leaving Egypt on that first trip. Almost everything that had happened to them had caused fear, but having the silver cup found in Benjamin's sack brought the greatest fear of all.

They finally admitted that they had been found out; that there was nothing they could say to defend themselves; that God had found out their iniquity.

God often uses fear to cause men to call upon Him. Fear probes, searches, warns, purifies, and keeps the heart tender and true. It keeps a person sensitive to God's will and causes him to shrink from sin. Fear, in its positive sense, actuates an intense desire to be true to God.

Many writers of Scripture commented about fear. The Apostle Paul told believers, "Work out your own salvation with fear and trembling. For it is God which worketh in you both to will and to do of his good pleasure" (Phil. 2:12,13). Of Noah it is said, "By faith Noah, being warned of God of things not seen as yet, moved with fear, prepared an ark to the saving of his house; by the which he condemned the world, and became heir of the righteousness which is by faith" (Heb. 11:7). Writing by inspiration, Jude said, "And others save with fear, pulling them out of the fire; hating even the garment spotted by the flesh" (v. 23).

It is because of such truths as these that it can be said that "the fear of the Lord is the beginning of wisdom" (Prov. 9:10). And thus it can also be said, "There is no fear in love; but perfect love casteth out fear" (I John 4:18).

Through Joseph the Lord's objective had now been reached. God had wanted to give perfect rest and peace to the brothers, but this was impossible as long as there was unconfessed sin in their lives. God used the avenues of conscience and fear to bring about this repentance. The brothers were being tested to see if they could forgive Benjamin who had brought them all of this trouble. If they had treated him in the spirit of the former days, as they had treated Joseph, they would have abandoned Benjamin to his fate. Had they done this, they could not have been forgiven. But Judah expressed their change of heart when he said he would rather stay in Egypt as a slave than go back and see his father die of a broken heart because of the loss of Benjamin.

The brothers had a forgiving spirit toward Benjamin. This is extremely important, for the Lord Jesus Christ said, "If ye forgive not men their trespasses, neither will your father forgive your trespasses" (Matt. 6:15). The four conditions of reconciliation had been met: conscience had been awakened, sin had been confessed, repentance had been made, and a new life had been evidenced. Joseph's brothers now had the right heart attitude. Because God's work had been accomplished in the lives of the brothers, Joseph was now free to reveal his identity.

Joseph Identifies Himself

The Scripture says that after Judah had ceased his pathetic pleading, "Joseph could not refrain himself before all them that stood by him; and he cried, Cause every man to go out from me. And there stood no man with him, while Joseph made himself known unto his brethren" (Gen. 45:1). Joseph did not have to hold his feelings back any longer. God's work had been accomplished in the lives of Joseph's brothers. However, had he not been able to control himself earlier, God's program would have been thwarted.

Even though his brothers were shepherds—and shepherds were an abomination to the Egyptians—Joseph was not ashamed to identify himself with them. His prosperity and Egyptian rank did not cause him to feel that he was above his brothers—self had been buried many years ago in the pit and in the prison cell.

So Joseph cried, "Cause every man to go out from me." This was a very delicate moment. His brothers had greatly sinned against him and he did not want to expose their sin to a group of onlookers. Also, this was an intimate time of reunion and it was most desirous that they be by themselves. His brothers especially needed time completely alone with Joseph.

Just as the brothers were alone with Joseph, so the believers will be alone with the Lord Jesus Christ when they are raptured from the earth. We are told of this time in I Thessalonians 4:16,17: "For the Lord himself shall descend from heaven with a shout, with the voice of the archangel, and with the trump of God: and the dead in Christ shall rise first: then we which are alive and remain shall be caught up together with them in the clouds, to meet the Lord in the air: and so shall we ever be with the Lord."

At the time of the Rapture, the Lord is going to take the believers out of this curious, sin-cursed world. The onlookers will be given no opportunity to see this intimate homecoming, when the believers will meet Jesus Christ face to face. Only the angels who have watched throughout the centuries will be allowed to see this great, glorious reunion of the Lord Jesus Christ with His Bride.

After Joseph had sent the onlookers from his presence, "he wept aloud: and the Egyptians and the house of Pharaoh heard" (Gen. 45:2). Joseph's pent-up emotions were released at last! It is difficult to imagine the reaction of the brothers when Joseph began to cry. All they had seen before was hardness in this ruler of Egypt, but now he was weeping uncontrollably before them.

"Joseph said unto his brethren, I am Joseph" (v. 3). Previously he had spoken to them through an interpreter, but now in their own language he said, "I am Joseph." Even though he spoke with deep emotion, his words must have hit them like a thunderbolt. Joseph! Had they been dealing with Joseph all this time? Yes, Joseph! Surely they had fallen into the lion's den themselves! It was unbelievable, but he must be Joseph for he was speaking to them in their own language. Everything was out in the open now; suddenly the pieces of the puzzle began to fall into place.

When Joseph disclosed his identity, "his brethren could not answer him; for they were troubled at his presence" (v. 3). They had reason to be troubled and terrified. Joseph was standing before them as one who had risen from the dead. Their faces reflected terror because of the possible consequences. They feared that now Joseph might retaliate for what they had done to him. He was now their master, and they stood hopeless and helpless in his presence. They could not think of what to say, because any act of self-defense would surely only bring them into deeper trouble.

Sent by God

Joseph recognized their hesitation and said to them, "Come near to me, I pray you. And they came near. And he said, I am Joseph your brother, whom ye sold into Egypt.

Now therefore be not grieved, nor angry with yourselves, that ye sold me hither: for God did send me before you to preserve life" (vv. 4,5).

Now it was out! There was no need to wonder further whether Joseph remembered their having sold him into Egypt. Even though Joseph admitted this, there was not the slightest word of reproach concerning the past. In fact, he hastened to comfort them by letting them know that it was not really they but God who had sent him to Egypt. Although this was the same person they had sold into slavery, he was significantly different. The lad had become a man. The years of bitter experiences had made their marks on him. He had a great depth of experience because of his many prolonged trials and altered circumstances. He readily acknowledged his relationship with them in the past because it was necessary to remind them of what they had done against him, but he assured them that God had used it for good.

When Joseph was brought from the dungeon to interpret Pharaoh's dreams, Joseph said, "It is not in me: God shall give Pharaoh an answer of peace" (41:16). Now Joseph told his brothers that the One responsible for his coming to Egypt was "not you . . . but God" (45:8). This is a truth we desperately need to see—that God moves behind the scenes to accomplish his purpose in our lives. For the Christian, things are not explained on a human basis—it is "not I, but Christ" (Gal. 2:20). It is only as we allow God to test, try and train us that He can accomplish His overall program and use us as He desires.

Joseph was precise in his understanding of why God had sent him to Egypt: "God did send me before you to preserve life" (Gen. 45:5). God had had a plan for Joseph but it was not for Joseph's sake alone that God had sent him to Egypt. It was to accomplish God's purpose of bringing Jacob's family to Egypt where they might become a great nation and later be able to return to the land of Canaan. Joseph went on to tell his brothers, "For these two years hath the famine been in the land: and yet there are five years, in the which there shall neither be earing [plowing] nor harvest. And God sent me before you to preserve you a posterity in the earth, and to save your lives by a great deliverance. So now it was not you that sent me hither, but God: and he hath made me a father to Pharaoh, and lord of all his house, and a ruler throughout all the land of Egypt" (vv. 6-8).

Even though there had been many bitter experiences and the brothers were personally responsible for their evil deeds, Joseph did not doubt that God had gloriously worked in spite of these circumstances to bring glory to Himself.

This principle of God's working was also seen in the crucifixion of the Lord Jesus Christ. In his sermon on the Day of Pentecost, Peter said, "Ye men of Israel, hear these words; Jesus of Nazareth, a man approved of God among you by miracles and wonders and signs, which God did by him in the midst of you, as ye yourselves also know: him, being delivered by the determinate counsel and foreknowledge of God, ye have taken, and by wicked hands have crucified and slain: whom God hath raised up, having loosed the pains of death: because it was not possible that he should be holden of it" (Acts 2:22-24). Men were responsible for their evil deeds, but God worked in spite of the circumstances to bring glory to Himself.

Joseph instructed his brothers to return home and tell his father that he was still alive. They were to tell Jacob of the position and glory that God had given Joseph in Egypt, and then they were to bring Jacob and all his family to Egypt where they could be cared for by Joseph.

Then followed one of the most touching scenes in the Bible: "He fell upon his brother Benjamin's neck, and wept; and Benjamin wept upon his neck. Moreover he kissed all his brethren, and wept upon them: and after that his brethren talked with him" (Gen. 45:14,15). Reconciliation had been made! Joseph first expressed his love to Benjamin and then to all the other brothers. "He kissed all his brethren"—those who had tied his hands and had mocked at his cries. After this expression of his love, "his brethren talked with him." The tears flowed freely and there was joy of communion.

I think this is much the way it will be when we meet the Lord face to face. When we see Him and His nail-pierced hands and truly realize all He has given for us, I think we shall shed tears. When we fully realize that He, in patience and long-suffering and compassion, made possible our salvation and that we are going to be in His presence forever, our joy will be inexpressible. When we fully realize our sinful condition, apart from Jesus Christ, we will shed tears of appreciation for His grace. Although I think there will be tears when we see Him face to face, there will not be tears for long because the Bible assures us that "God shall wipe away all tears from their eyes; and there shall be no more death, neither sorrow, nor crying, neither shall there be any more pain: for the former things are passed away" (Rev. 21:4). What a wonderful God we have!

Joseph was not ashamed of his brothers. Only a person indwelt by the Holy Spirit could endure all that Joseph did and still love his brothers. Joseph's eyes were fixed on God, not on circumstances. He wanted to forget the past and the years of broken fellowship with his brothers and now move forward in harmony with them.

This reminds us of the Apostle Paul who, when referring to the past, said, "But what things were gain to me, those I counted loss for Christ" (Phil. 3:7). The epitomy of Paul's desire is seen in his words, "That I may know him, and the power of his resurrection, and the fellowship of his sufferings, being made conformable unto his death; if by any means I might attain unto the resurrection of the dead. Not as though I had already attained, either were already perfect: but I follow after, if that I may apprehend that for which also I am apprehended of Christ Jesus. Brethren, I count not myself to have apprehended: but this one thing I do, forgetting those things which are behind, and reaching forth unto those things which are before, I press toward the mark for the prize of the high calling of God in Christ Jesus" (vv. 10-14).

Joseph's power and rank never tempted him to take vengeance on his brothers because of their cruelty to him.

One of the hardest trials that can come to any person is that of being ill-used by his own flesh and blood. How extremely difficult it is when your own family does not understand your desires! There is scarcely anything more trying in life than being misunderstood, having motives misconstrued and intentions distorted. Under such circumstances, the reaction of the natural man is to retaliate—to return bitterness for bitterness. But Joseph had matured in these areas also. Long before Christ taught returning good for evil, this Old Testament believer demonstrated it by his life. He loved his enemies and did good to those who despitefully used him. Joseph's true character is nowhere more clearly seen than in his lofty, noble and generous treatment of his unworthy brothers. His brothers could not really comprehend such a forgiving spirit. In fact, as we will see later, the brothers were still suspicious that Joseph might retaliate against them even after their father died. Joseph was deeply grieved because of their lack of confidence in his forgiving spirit.

Joseph never saw himself as one who needed to seek revenge. He understood clearly the principle that was later stated in Hebrews 10:30: "Vengeance belongeth unto me, I will recompense, saith the Lord. And again, the Lord shall judge his people." Joseph's many years of trials caused him to be patient and understanding even when those he dearly loved misunderstood him. Instead of seeking revenge, he wept. His heart went out to those he loved so much.

Jesus also wept for those He dearly loved. He came into the world He had created, but His own people would not receive Him. Instead, they demanded that He be crucified for claiming to be the Son of God. Some of the most pathetic words ever spoken by the Lord Jesus are recorded in Luke 13:34,35: "O Jerusalem, Jerusalem, which killest the prophets, and stonest them that are sent unto thee; how often would I have gathered thy children together, as a hen doth gather her brood under her wings, and ye would not! Behold, your house is left unto you desolate: and verily I say unto you, Ye shall not see me, until the time come when ye

shall say, Blessed is he that cometh in the name of the Lord."
Jesus wept over Jerusalem.

Joseph's heart was tender because he realized God had
been working out His purpose all along. After revealing
himself to his brothers, Joseph was able to say, "God sent me
before you to preserve you a posterity in the earth" (Gen.
45:7). Years later he was still able to say, "God planned it for
good" (50:20, Berkeley).

Joseph had passed his tests with flying colors. He had not
become embittered by adversity nor elated by prosperity.
Nor had he become vindictive toward his brothers. He had
successfully passed his tests because he was more concerned
about God and others than he was about himself. This was
also true later of Timothy of whom the Apostle Paul told the
Philippians: "For I have no man likeminded, who will
naturally care for your state. For all seek their own, not the
things which are Jesus Christ's. But ye know the proof of
him, that, as a son with the father, he hath served with me in
the gospel" (Phil. 2:20-22).

Joseph submitted himself to God so that he could learn
the lessons God wanted him to learn and be used as God
desired. In the midst of the tests, Joseph did not know what
God was trying to accomplish in his life, but he was
confident that everything was in God's hands and that
someday he would understand.

Chapter 8

Emigration

Because the famine "was over all the face of the earth" (Gen. 41:56), Joseph commissioned his brothers to return to Canaan and bring their father to Egypt. Joseph said, "Haste ye, and go up to my father, and say unto him, Thus saith thy son Joseph, God hath made me lord of all Egypt: come down unto me, tarry not: and thou shalt dwell in the land of Goshen, and thou shalt be near unto me, thou, and thy children, and thy children's children, and thy flocks, and thy herds, and all that thou hast: and there will I nourish thee; for yet there are five years of famine; lest thou, and thy household, and all that thou hast, come to poverty. And, behold, your eyes see, and the eyes of my brother Benjamin, that it is my mouth that speaketh unto you. And ye shall tell my father of all my glory in Egypt, and of all that ye have seen; and ye shall haste and bring down my father hither" (45:9-13).

Joseph's brothers were not to describe these things in their own words, but they were to communicate the actual words of Joseph. And notice that the first words they were to quote Joseph as saying were, "God hath...." (v. 9). Joseph took no credit for his exalted position in Egypt. It was clear to him that this had come about because of God's working, and he was quick to emphasize this fact. It was not just a humble admission; it was a positive declaration to the glory of God.

Although his relatives were shepherds, Joseph was not ashamed to be associated with them. In fact, he was anxious that his brothers return to Canaan and bring their father to Egypt as soon as possible. Joseph was unashamed of his relatives because he was a man of God, indwelt by the Holy Spirit.

The brothers were not to keep the good news to themselves—they were to tell their father and bring him to Egypt. However, telling their father about these things meant they would have to admit their sin of selling Joseph into slavery over 20 years earlier. All of these years they had kept the secret from their father, and though he may have been suspicious that they had done something underhanded, he never knew for sure. But now they were to face the facts and make things right with their father.

So it is in our lives when we become right with God: we may have to go to some people and straighten things out. Fellowship with God is evidenced by our seeking to restore fellowship with those we have sinned against.

Joseph commissioned his brothers to tell their father three things: Joseph is alive; he has an exalted position; and he wants to receive you and your family to himself. They were to conceal nothing that Joseph told them to say.

Our Responsibility

So it is with us: we are not to conceal the Good News. We are commissioned to proclaim the gospel to every creature. We are to tell them that Jesus Christ is alive, that He has an exalted position, and that He wants them to come into right relationship with Him. The humiliation, death, resurrection and exaltation of Christ are set forth in Philippians 2:5-9: "Let this mind be in you, which was also in Christ Jesus: who, being in the form of God, thought it not robbery to be equal with God: but made himself of no reputation, and took upon him the form of a servant, and was made in the likeness of men: and being found in fashion as a man, he humbled himself, and became obedient unto death, even the death of the cross. Wherefore God also hath highly exalted him, and given him a name which is above every name."

Just as Joseph's brothers were to tell the news of their having been reconciled to Joseph, so the Christian is to tell everyone the news that reconciliation to God has been made possible through the Lord Jesus Christ. The Apostle Paul wrote, "Therefore if any man be in Christ, he is a new creature: old things are passed away; behold, all things are become new. And all things are of God, who hath reconciled us to himself by Jesus Christ, and hath given to us the ministry of reconciliation; to wit, that God was in Christ, reconciling the world unto himself, not imputing their trespasses unto them; and hath committed unto us the word of reconciliation" (II Cor. 5:17-19). Through His death, Christ made reconciliation with God possible. We who know Christ as Saviour are commissioned to tell others about Him. He even gives us the words of reconciliation. What a shame it is that so few Christians are aggressively telling others about the good news of salvation. How can we be so rebellious in refusing to do what God has told us to do—to tell others? Have we no love for God and for those who need Him? Have we no fear of giving account to Jesus Christ?

In this same chapter in II Corinthians, Paul wrote, "For we must all appear before the judgment seat of Christ; that every one may receive the things done in his body, according to that he hath done, whether it be good or bad. Knowing therefore the terror of the Lord, we persuade men" (vv. 10,11). Every believer is to be a witness. Christ said, "But ye shall receive power, after that the Holy Ghost is come upon you: and ye shall be witnesses unto me both in Jerusalem, and in all Judea, and in Samaria, and unto the uttermost part of the earth" (Acts 1:8). The Holy Spirit came on the Day of Pentecost and since that time, every believer has been indwelt by Him. As we yield to His control, he will enable us to be effective witnesses of Jesus Christ.

We talk much about the rebellion of our youth today, but we are reaping what we have sown in our own rebellion against God. We have not been faithful witnesses in telling what we have seen and experienced. We have not been faithful in telling others that Jesus Christ is alive, that He has an exalted position with God, and that He desires them to be reconciled to Himself. We have been commissioned to share this news, and the day is coming when we shall reckon with Him on our obedience to His commission. This does not mean that every Christian must be a preacher or a missionary, but it does mean that we should be faithful in communicating to others with whom we are associated in our daily walk that they can be reconciled to God by receiving Jesus Christ as Saviour. Let us not be rebellious by refusing to proclaim the good news of salvation.

Because Joseph knew God's promises which He had made to Abraham, Isaac and Jacob, he now realized that God was using him to preserve this chosen family so it could become a great nation. Thus Joseph urged his brothers to bring their father to Egypt. They were to dwell in the land of Goshen. Joseph said, "There will I nourish thee" (Gen. 45:11). Although the brothers had sinned against him, his heart was not hardened toward them nor toward the rest of his family. He realized God had appointed him to be a saviour of the family in physically preserving them at this time.

The Scriptures say that "the fame thereof was heard in Pharaoh's house, saying, Joseph's brethren are come: and it pleased Pharaoh well, and his servants. And Pharaoh said unto Joseph, Say unto thy brethren, This do ye; lade your beasts, and go, get you unto the land of Canaan; and take your father and your households, and come unto me: and I will give you the good of the land of Egypt, and ye shall eat the fat of the land. Now thou art commanded, this do ye; take you wagons out of the land of Egypt for your little ones, and for your wives, and bring your father, and come. Also regard not your stuff; for the good of all the land of Egypt is your's" (vv. 16-20).

Pharaoh reaffirmed what Joseph had said to his brothers. This was significant because Joseph might have been accused of being partial to his own family. However, God protected Joseph and his reputation by causing Pharaoh to give the same orders for them to come to Egypt. So Joseph's brothers returned to their father after provisions had been given to them, according to the words of Joseph and Pharaoh.

Jacob's Unbelief

When they reached home, they told their father, "Joseph is yet alive, and he is governor over all the land of Egypt" (v. 26). Jacob was so surprised by the news that it was impossible for him to believe it. The Scriptures say, "Jacob's heart fainted, for he believed them not" (v. 26). Earlier, when it was demanded that Benjamin go to Egypt with the brothers so they would be able to see Joseph, Jacob had said, "All these things are against me" (42:36). He did not realize that just the opposite was true—all those things were really working together for good. God had patiently worked to accomplish His will. When God undertakes a program, He continues with it until it is finished. The Apostle Paul wrote: "Being confident of this very thing, that he which hath begun a good work in you will perform it until the day of Jesus Christ" (Phil. 1:6).

Although at first Jacob was overwhelmed with the news and did not believe his sons, "they told him all the words of Joseph, which he had said unto them: and when he saw the wagons which Joseph had sent to carry him, the spirit of Jacob their father revived: and Israel [Jacob] said, It is enough; Joseph my son is yet alive: I will go and see him before I die" (Gen. 45:27,28).

When Jacob saw the wagons, he believed. Some say, "Seeing is believing." However, the Bible says quite the opposite is true. The disciple Thomas would not believe that the Saviour had risen from the dead. When the other disciples told him they had seen the risen Lord, Thomas said, "Except I shall see in his hands the print of the nails, and put my finger into the print of the nails, and thrust my hand into his side, I will not believe" (John 20:25). Eight days later when the Lord appeared to the disciples, He said to Thomas, "Reach hither thy finger, and behold my hands; and reach

hither thy hand, and thrust it into my side: and be not
faithless, but believing" (v. 27). Thomas responded by
exclaiming, "My Lord and my God" (v. 28). But notice what
Jesus then said: "Thomas, because thou hast seen me, thou
hast believed: blessed are they that have not seen, and yet
have believed" (v. 29).

Abraham was a prime Old Testament example of one
who believed without seeing. Of him it is said, "Who against
hope believed in hope, that he might become the father of
many nations; according to that which was spoken, So shall
thy seed be. And being not weak in faith, he considered not
his own body now dead, when he was about an hundred
years old, neither yet the deadness of Sarah's womb: he
staggered not at the promise of God through unbelief; but
was strong in faith, giving glory to God; and being fully
persuaded that, what he had promised, he was able also to
perform. And therefore it was imputed to him for
righteousness" (Rom. 4:18-22). The principle for believers
was stated by the Apostle Paul: "For we walk by faith, not
by sight" (II Cor. 5:7).

Jacob Seeks God's Will

Although Jacob was persuaded that Joseph was alive, he
did not go to see him without consulting God. Jacob had
passed through many severe tests in his lifetime, and it had
been harder for him to learn the lessons of God than it had
for his son Joseph. But Jacob had finally learned the lessons
even though it had taken him many years. So even though
Joseph had invited him down to Egypt, and though the
circumstances seemed to be just right to go, Jacob was not
about to do this without being sure of God's will.

We also need to be assured that God has a plan for our lives.
It is not necessary that we understand every detail in the plan,
but at least we need to realize that God is working and that
He knows what He is doing. When Lazarus was sick, his
sisters—Mary and Martha—sent for Jesus, saying, "Lord,
behold, he whom thou lovest is sick" (John 11:3). However,

Jesus purposely waited until Lazarus died before He came to Bethany to visit the home. The sisters were heartbroken and both said to Jesus, "Lord, if thou hadst been here, my brother had not died" (vv. 21,32). Jesus went to the grave and said, "Take ye away the stone" (v. 39). Martha immediately spoke up saying, "Lord, by this time he stinketh: for he hath been dead four days" (v. 39). Then Jesus made a statement to Martha that we need to apply to our lives. He said, "Said I not unto thee, that, if thou wouldest believe, thou shouldest see the glory of God?" (v. 40).

Jesus was asking Martha to trust Him *because He knew what He was doing.* He had purposely delayed His coming because God was glorified more through the raising of Lazarus from the dead than He would have been through curing his illness. So too, we need to trust God completely and have the confidence that He knows what He is doing in our lives.

The Bible says that Jacob "took his journey with all that he had, and came to Beer-sheba, and offered sacrifices unto the God of his father Isaac" (Gen. 46:1). It was at Beersheba that Jacob's father, Isaac, had built an altar to God. To Jacob this seemed a very special place for worshiping God. He went that far with his family, then stopped there to know the mind of the Lord about proceeding further.

While at Beersheba, "God spake unto Israel [Jacob] in the visions of the night, and said, Jacob, Jacob. And he said, Here am I" (v. 2). Jacob was ready for the Lord to speak to him and immediately responded, "Here am I." He was anxious to hear all that God had to say to him.

God told Jacob, "I am God, the God of thy father: fear not to go down into Egypt; for I will there make of thee a great nation: I will go down with thee into Egypt; and I will also surely bring thee up again: and Joseph shall put his hand upon thine eyes" (vv. 3,4). In these verses we see that God told Jacob: "I am God." In this name resides all finality. Jacob had learned to know this and to follow His directions without question. God told Jacob: "Fear not to go down into Egypt." This was the encouragement Jacob wanted to hear, for he would not go to Egypt without God's direction.

God then gave Jacob a fourfold promise: "I will there make of thee a great nation: I will go down with thee into Egypt; and I will also surely bring thee up again: and Joseph shall put his hand upon thine eyes" (vv. 3,4).

God made it clear to Jacob that going to Egypt was only a temporary move. This was not an emergency step in God's program—He was not taken by surprise in any way. God had a definite purpose in view and that was to make this family into a great nation. At this time they were only a handful of people, but God was going to multiply them in Egypt where they could keep their uniqueness and not be amalgamated with others. Growth in number was slow at first but they multiplied rapidly.

Fulfilling Prophecy

God also began slowly with Abraham when He promised him a son. Abraham had to wait 25 years for the son of God's choice. During those years God taught Abraham many spiritual principles. Later, Abraham's son Isaac had two sons—also after a long period of waiting. There were many principles that Isaac needed to learn too. Thus there had not been rapid growth among the Hebrews even though God had promised that they would be as the stars of the heavens.

When one considers the promises God made to Abraham, it is evident that His instructions to Jacob to go to Egypt were not of recent development. God was not caught off guard; Egypt was part of His overall plan for His people. God had told Abraham: "Know of a surety that thy seed shall be a stranger in a land that is not theirs, and shall serve them; and they shall afflict them four hundred years; and also that nation, whom they shall serve, will I judge: and afterward shall they come out with great substance. And thou shalt go to thy fathers in peace; thou shalt be buried in a good old age. But in the fourth generation they shall come hither again: for the iniquity of the Amorites is not yet full" (15:13-16).

The time had now come to fulfill this prophecy spoken to Abraham. God was sending this family to Egypt where He would make it into a great nation. Because shepherds were an abomination to the Egyptians, Jacob's descendants would remain separate from these idolatrous people. And because Joseph was prime minister there, Jacob's descendants would have no physical want—he had promised to nourish them there (45:11). In Egypt they would be free from the danger of attack and destruction, which they constantly faced in Canaan. They would have room for their multiplying numbers in Egypt. They would live under an established and well-ordered government—a great contrast to what they had in Canaan. In Egypt they would have the advantage of the training and discipline they would need as they became a great nation. Joseph's brothers had lived as if they were responsible only to themselves. When they had decided earlier that they did not want Joseph around anymore, they sold him into slavery. They lived as if they were answerable to no one. So now God was bringing them into a country where there would be training and discipline.

Later, when Moses rose to be the emancipator of Israel, he also learned basic principles of leadership in Egypt.

Jacob Goes to Egypt

After God had given Jacob instructions, "Jacob rose up from Beer-sheba: and the sons of Israel carried Jacob their father, and their little ones, and their wives, in the wagons which Pharaoh had sent to carry him. And they took their cattle, and their goods, which they had gotten in the land of Canaan, and came into Egypt, Jacob, and all his seed with him" (46:5,6). The record says that "all the souls that came with Jacob into Egypt, which came out of his loins, besides Jacob's sons' wives, all the souls were threescore and six" (v. 26). When one includes Jacob, as well as Joseph and his two sons, the total number in the family was 70. This is indicated in verse 27: "And the sons of Joseph, which were born him in Egypt, were two souls: all the souls of the house of Jacob, which came into Egypt, were threescore and ten." Out of 70 people God was to make a mighty nation.

When Jacob and his family arrived in Goshen, "Joseph made ready his chariot, and went up to meet Israel his father, to Goshen, and presented himself unto him; and he fell on his neck, and wept on his neck a good while" (v. 29). Again Joseph demonstrated that he was not ashamed to be associated with his family even though shepherds were an abomination to the Egyptians. What a tender scene it must have been when Joseph met his father and embraced him, weeping for joy. Jacob said to Joseph, "Now let me die, since I have seen thy face, because thou art yet alive" (v. 30).

It was at this time that we see Joseph's wise strategy as he prepared his family for their meeting with Pharaoh: "Joseph said unto his brethren, and unto his father's house, I will go up, and shew Pharaoh, and say unto him, My brethren, and my father's house, which were in the land of Canaan, are come unto me; and the men are shepherds, for their trade hath been to feed cattle; and they have brought their flocks, and their herds, and all that they have. And it shall come to pass, when Pharaoh shall call you, and shall say, What is your occupation? that ye shall say, Thy servants' trade hath been about cattle from our youth even until now, both we, and also our fathers: that ye may dwell in the land of Goshen; for every shepherd is an abomination unto the Egyptians" (vv. 31-34).

Joseph's plan was to consult with Pharaoh at once. By bringing these matters before Pharaoh, Joseph was preventing the possibility that someone would accuse him of favoritism. Also, when Pharaoh gave the word, the chiefs of the people would not thwart Joseph's plan. Later, it was in God's plan to have another Pharaoh—who did not know Joseph—afflict the Israelites in order to cause them to want to leave Egypt.

Joseph brought some of his family before Pharaoh. After Pharaoh asked regarding their occupation, he told Joseph, "Thy father and thy brethren are come unto thee: the land of Egypt is before thee; in the best of the land make thy father and brethren to dwell; in the land of Goshen let him dwell: and if thou knowest any men of activity [able men] among them, then make them rulers over my cattle" (47:5,6).

Then Joseph brought his father into Pharaoh. After this, "Joseph placed his father and his brethren, and gave them a possession in the land of Egypt, in the best of the land, in the land of Rameses, as Pharaoh had commanded. And Joseph nourished his father, and his brethren and all his father's household, with bread, according to their families" (vv. 11,12). Joseph's family was now safe in the land of Goshen. He must have rejoiced as he reflected on how God's hand had been in all his personal afflictions and his exaltation in order that his family might be preserved. He had experienced the reality of what God had caused him to dream over 20 years ago.

Joseph had experienced the fulfillment of the truths stated in Psalm 37. He had delighted himself in the Lord, and the Lord had given him the desires of his heart" (v. 4). He had waited upon the Lord and had inherited the earth (v. 9). Being meek, he had delighted himself in the abundance of peace (v. 11). Because he was a good man, his steps had been ordered by the Lord and he had delighted in the Lord's way (v. 23). He had waited on the Lord and had kept His way; therefore, he had been exalted to inherit the land and had seen the wicked cut off (v. 34). He had been a perfect (mature) man; therefore, his end was peace (v. 37). We need to apply this Psalm to ourselves.

The Scriptures say that "Israel [Jacob] dwelt in the land of Egypt, in the country of Goshen; and they had possessions therein, and grew, and multiplied exceedingly. And Jacob lived in the land of Egypt seventeen years: so the whole age of Jacob was an hundred forty and seven years. And the time drew nigh that Israel must die: and he called his son Joseph, and said unto him, If now I have found grace in thy sight, put, I pray thee, thy hand under my thigh, and deal kindly and truly with me; bury me not, I pray thee, in Egypt: but I will lie with my fathers, and thou shalt carry me out of Egypt, and bury me in their buryingplace. And he said, I will do as thou hast said. And he said, Swear unto me. And he sware unto him. And Israel bowed himself upon the bed's head" (Gen. 47:27-31).

God had promised Jacob that He would make a great nation of him in Egypt and that they would return to the land. Jacob's faith in God's promises was revealed in that he asked Joseph to bury him back in Canaan. His request must have had a great impact on Joseph because Joseph later requested the same thing for himself (50:24,25).

God had fulfilled His purpose through Joseph. Joseph had been used to preserve the posterity of the Hebrews. They were now safe in the land of Goshen. Years later, when it was time to lead the Israelites out of Egypt, God used another man—Moses. God has limited Himself to working through people to accomplish His will.

Remaining Years of Famine

Joseph was a very wise ruler because God was with him and gave him great wisdom. During the seven years of plenty, Joseph set plans into operation that would conserve food for the seven years of famine. When the famine came, it was not only in Egypt but also in other parts of the world. Even after his family came to the land of Goshen, it is said that "there was no bread in all the land; for the famine was very sore, so that the land of Egypt and all the land of Canaan fainted by reason of the famine" (47:13).

During the remaining years of famine, Joseph received money for food; and when the money was gone, he received livestock for food. The people "brought their cattle unto Joseph, and Joseph gave them bread in exchange for horses, and for the flocks, and for the cattle of the herds, and for the asses: and he fed them with bread for all their cattle for that year" (v. 17). Later, Joseph received land for food: "Joseph bought all the land of Egypt for Pharaoh; for the Egyptians sold every man his field, because the famine prevailed over them: so the land became Pharaoh's" (v. 20).

Joseph evidenced wise leadership when he made the people tenants on Pharaoh's land and gave them seed to sow. A fifth of anything that grew was to be Pharaoh's. Joseph instructed, "It shall come to pass in the increase, that ye shall give the fifth part unto Pharaoh, and four parts shall be your own, for seed of the field, and for your food, and for them of your households, and for food for your little ones" (v. 24).

The people were very grateful. They recognized that Joseph had saved their lives and they willingly submitted to being Pharaoh's servants. They said to Joseph, "Thou hast saved our lives: let us find grace in the sight of my lord, and we will be Pharaoh's servants" (v. 25). In a physical sense, Joseph was the saviour of the world because he had kept the people from starvation.

God's Ultimate Rule

From these incidents it is evident that the operation of the Spirit is not limited to things that are purely spiritual in nature. The Spirit also works to accomplish the purpose of God in the nations of the world. Ultimately, God rules the nations of the world. The words of Jehoshaphat were true when he said, "O Lord God of our fathers, art thou not God in heaven? and rulest not thou over all the kingdoms of the heathen [nations]? and in thine hand is there not power and might, so that none is able to withstand thee?" (II Chron. 20:6). When we understand that God ultimately rules the nations of the world, we will not be so discouraged about today's world conditions. It is true that many things are being done which do not honor God, but He is allowing men to see that they are unable to rule themselves. Even when the Antichrist appears on the scene during the Tribulation and presents a plan for world rule, God will show that it will not work because He is not included.

Daniel saw God's ultimate rulership of the nations in the case of Nebuchadnezzar. In one of his dreams,

Nebuchadnezzar saw a great tree which Daniel later explained to be Nebuchadnezzar himself (Dan. 4:10,14,20-22). In the dream the command was given to cut down the tree but leave the stump of his roots in the earth and to "let his heart be changed from man's, and let a beast's heart be given unto him; and let seven times [years] pass over him" (v. 16). Then there was given these great words, which show how God works in the nations: "This matter is by the decree of the watchers, and the demand by the word of the holy ones: to the intent that the living may know that the most High ruleth in the kingdom of men, and giveth it to whomsoever he will, and setteth up over it the basest of men" (v. 17).

The dream was later fulfilled when Nebuchadnezzar became temporarily insane because of the intense pride of his heart. A year after his dream Nebuchadnezzar was walking in the palace of the kingdom of Babylon and he said, "Is not this great Babylon, that I have built for the house of the kingdom by the might of my power, and for the honour of my majesty? While the word was in the king's mouth, there fell a voice from heaven, saying, O king Nebuchadnezzar, to thee it is spoken; The kingdom is departed from thee. And they shall drive thee from men, and thy dwelling shall be with the beasts of the field: they shall make thee to eat grass as oxen, and seven times [years] shall pass over thee, until thou know that the most High ruleth in the kingdom of men, and giveth it to whomsoever he will" (vv. 30-32). Nebuchadnezzar had to learn the lesson that God sets up rulers and that He takes them down at His will.

The Apostle Paul wrote: "Let every soul be subject unto the higher powers. For there is no power but of God: the powers that be are ordained of God" (Rom. 13:1). Realizing that God ultimately rules the nations, we need to pray that leaders will recognize their responsibility to God. The Apostle Paul also said, "I exhort therefore, that, first of all, supplications, prayers, intercessions, and giving of thanks, be made for all men; for kings, and for all that are in authority; that we may lead a quiet and peaceable life in all godliness and honesty. For this is good and acceptable in the sight of

God our Saviour: who will have all men to be saved, and to come unto the knowledge of the truth" (I Tim. 2:1-4).

Success Without Compromise

Joseph demonstrated that it is possible for a believer to succeed in business and still be true to his spiritual convictions. However, we must be careful not to make success in the world the determining factor in deciding whether a person is a good Christian or not. There are many Christians who are walking in fellowship with God but who have not experienced success according to the world's standards. But it is also true that a Christian does not have to compromise his standards in order to become a success. If he compromises his convictions, God will not be able to use him—and even the world will have serious reservations about him. Joseph was advanced because it was obvious he would not compromise his convictions.

Joseph might be spoken of as "not slothful in business; fervent in spirit; serving the Lord" (Rom. 12:11). Joseph's religion affected every area of his life. The result was that he glorified God and became a great influence in extending the knowledge of God wherever he went. This should also be true of us. Whatever we do and wherever we go, we should make known God and His gospel of salvation.

Joseph did not leave his close associates wondering about his relationship with God. Whether he was working for Potiphar, spending time in prison, or serving as prime minister under Pharaoh, the influence of Joseph's life had a great impact on those he was with. They witnessed firsthand his loyalty to his God, and in his life they saw God's power manifested. Joseph did not have the type of belief that affected him only one day of the week. His relationship with God vitally touched every area of his life every day of the week.

As we seek to glorify God in daily living, there are questions that often arise as to whether or not it is right to do certain things. There are three verses that are especially helpful at such times. Colossians 3:17 says, "Whatsoever ye do in word or deed, do all in the name of the Lord Jesus, giving thanks to God and the Father by him." When you are faced with doing a certain thing, can you do it in the name of the Lord Jesus Christ? This does not mean that the activity must be some "spiritual" activity, but it must not be an activity that dishonors Christ's name.

Another key verse on this subject is Colossians 3:23: "Whatsoever ye do, do it heartily, as to the Lord, and not unto men." If you cannot do something with all your heart, as unto the Lord, you should not do it.

Another verse is I Corinthians 10:31: "Whether therefore ye eat, or drink, or whatsoever ye do, do all to the glory of God." If you will not ultimately bring about God's glory by doing something, then you should not do it. When these three verses and their principles are applied to life's questions, they will keep you in the center of God's will and favor.

Chapter 9

Joseph's Remaining Years

After the famine was over, Joseph lived about 66 more years. Jacob lived only about 10 or 11 more years. Little is said about either of them during these years. However, there was one highly significant thing that occurred before Jacob's death. Jacob said to Joseph, "God Almighty appeared unto me at Luz in the land of Canaan, and blessed me, and said unto me, Behold, I will make thee fruitful, and multiply thee, and I will make of thee a multitude of people; and will give this land to thy seed after thee for an everlasting possession. And now thy two sons, Ephraim and Manasseh, which were born unto thee in the land of Egypt before I came unto thee into Egypt, are mine; as Reuben and Simeon, they shall be mine. And thy issue, which thou begettest after them, shall be thine, and shall be called after the name of their brethren in their inheritance" (Gen. 48:3-6).

Jacob said that his grandsons, Ephraim and Manasseh, would be counted among his own sons, which was significant as far as the inheritance was concerned. Although Reuben was the firstborn of Leah, he had lost the birthright because of the gross sin of lying with his father's concubine. This birthright was then passed on to Joseph, the firstborn of Rachel. The birthright, having come to Joseph, was then given to his sons. This was later referred to in I Chronicles 5:1,2: "Now the sons of Reuben the firstborn of Israel, (for he was the firstborn; but, forasmuch as he defiled his father's bed, his birthright was given unto the sons of Joseph the son of Israel: and the genealogy is not to be reckoned after the birthright. For Judah prevailed above his brethren, and of him came the chief ruler; but the birthright was Joseph's)."

Joseph had received the double portion of inheritance and his two sons were numbered among the 12 tribes of Israel as the recipients.

The secret of Joseph's life was summed up in his own words when his brothers first came to Egypt. He told them, "This do, and live; for I fear God" (Gen. 42:18). The last three words of this statement were the key to his life—"I fear God."

To fear God does not just mean that one is afraid of God; it means that one has a reverential trust in God. This includes fear to the extent that we should fear lest we do something that will displease God, but it is much more than just being afraid of Him.

God was an ever-present reality to Joseph. God dominated every aspect of his life. This was why Joseph could be so greatly used—his trust was in God, not in himself nor in circumstances. The thing that was uppermost in Joseph's mind was not his own needs and wants but that he should please God in everything.

This is our need also—to put Christ first in everything. When we do this, He will take care of the rest. The Lord Jesus Christ said, "But seek ye first the kingdom of God, and his righteousness; and all these things shall be added unto you" (Matt. 6:33). When we put Christ first, we will be strongly devoted to the Word of God. These two are almost inseparable. When you go the Lord Jesus Christ, He directs you to the Word; when you go to the Word, it directs you to the Lord Jesus Christ.

There were four things that were particularly significant about Joseph's secret—"I fear God." First, he learned this secret early in his life while he was still at home. This shows us the importance of giving our children the spiritual training they need while they are yet young. In the discussion of Joseph's earlier years, it was pointed out that he had a far different training than his older brothers. His older brothers received their training before their father, Jacob, was really tender to the things of God. They did not receive much of the kind of spiritual training they needed. But Joseph was still in his tender years when his father met God at Peniel. Jacob became a changed man and this greatly affected Joseph's early training.

Second, the secret of Joseph's life was developed by his loyalty and obedience in the routine of daily duty. It did not matter whether things were small or large—he was faithful. Because he was faithful in little things, God gave him opportunity to be faithful in much. "Faithful" is a word that well describes all of Joseph's life. Above all, he was faithful to God who was the source, center, and springboard for every word and action in his life.

Third, the secret of Joseph's life was proved by the results. God honored His servant for his simple trust and confidence and justified his actions in his home life, slavery, prison, and in Pharaoh's court.

No life which is lived for the glory of God is without God's vindication. Such a life may not be vindicated immediately, as Joseph's was not, but God will eventually justify the actions of those who live for His glory. God's Word promises: "Commit thy way unto the Lord; trust also in him; and he shall bring it to pass. And he shall bring forth thy righteousness as the light, and thy judgment as the noonday" (Ps. 37:5,6). I keep coming back to this portion of Scripture because it is crucial in this regard.

Fourth, the secret of Joseph's life was made effectual in daily living by faith. Faith in God was evidenced throughout all his life, even when he faced death. The divine commentary is that "by faith Joseph, when he died, made mention of the departing of the children of Israel; and gave commandment concerning his bones" (Heb. 11:22). Faith is powerful and always brings results. W. H. Griffith Thomas, a great man of God of another generation, said that faith "is man's complete response to God's revelation. It links man's life to God, and provides him with a simple yet all-powerful secret of a life of power, purity and progress" (*Genesis*, p. 499). God looks for faith—He puts His power into operation in our lives when we exercise faith.

Faith's Characteristics

W. H. Griffith Thomas used six Rs in summarizing what faith does: Faith realizes, relies, responds, receives, rests, and rejoices.

First, "faith *realizes* God's presence and lives in it moment by moment" (*Ibid.*). It never says, "God, why are You so far away?"

Second, "faith *relies* on God's Word" (*Ibid.*). It believes that God will do what He has said He will do. It does not doubt God's Word.

Third, "faith *responds* to God's call, and obeys with readiness and loyalty" (*Ibid.*). Faith that is not active—that does not produce something—is not actually faith at all. True faith in God and His Word responds to Him and obeys. Faith says, "Here am I, Lord. I put myself at Your disposal."

Fourth, "faith *receives* God's grace, and finds it all-sufficient for daily needs" (*Ibid.*). Whatever your need is, God will be that to you. Thus we read: "Of him are ye in Christ Jesus, who of God is made unto us wisdom, and righteousness, and sanctification, and redemption" (I Cor. 1:30). Even God's Old Testament name "Jehovah" shows He will be to us whatever we need, for it actually means "I am." He ever lives to be whatever we need.

Fifth, "faith *rests* in God's will, and believes to see the goodness of the Lord in the land of the living" (*Ibid.*). Faith rests—it simply relaxes in God. It is not a type of rest which lacks something to do; rather it is the type of rest that releases anxiety and worry because it simply and completely trusts in God. Even when things go wrong, faith rests in God.

Sixth, "faith *rejoices* in God's protection, and knows that it shall not be put to shame" (*Ibid.*). It rejoices in what God is doing and in the way God takes care of His own.

Hebrews 11:6 is a key verse concerning faith: "Without faith it is impossible to please him: for he that cometh to

God must believe that he is, and that he is a rewarder of them that diligently seek him." Do you want victory in your life? Do you want to please God in everything you do? Then remember, "without faith it is impossible to please him."

Another key verse concerning faith is I John 5:4: "For whatsoever is born of God overcometh the world: and this is the victory that overcometh the world, even our faith." Believing that God *is*, that He is present, that He indwells us, that He is working in us, and that He will work out His life through us as we are obedient, will give us the victory we are looking for.

Joseph's Brothers Fear Again

A lack of faith was demonstrated by Joseph's brothers after the death of their father. Joseph had assured the brothers that all had been forgiven. Even though the brothers were responsible for their evil deed of selling Joseph into slavery, Joseph had told them, "So now it was not you that sent me hither, but God" (Gen. 45:8). The brothers had seemed to accept Joseph's statement, but after their father died they began to wonder again if Joseph might retaliate. They said, "Joseph will peradventure hate us, and will certainly requite us all the evil which we did unto him. And they sent a messenger unto Joseph, saying, Thy father did command before he died, saying, So shall ye say unto Joseph, Forgive, I pray thee now, the trespass of thy brethren, and their sin: for they did unto thee evil: and now, we pray thee, forgive the trespass of the servants of the God of thy father" (50:15-17).

The brothers were pleading that Joseph might take heed to their father's words and forgive them for what they had done. Notice Joseph's reaction when he heard these words from his brothers: "And Joseph wept when they spake unto him" (v. 17). Joseph wept because his brothers refused to believe him. It was heartbreaking for him to realize that his brothers had so little faith in him.

This gives us a small picture of how God's heart is broken when we do not take Him at His word. God can be trusted; therefore, let us exercise faith and take Him at His word.

We see the emotions of God when we read of how Jesus sorrowed over Jerusalem (Matt. 23:37). He grieved because they rejected Him—they refused to place their faith in Him. Jesus cried, "O Jerusalem, Jerusalem, thou that killest the prophets, and stonest them which are sent unto thee, how often would I have gathered thy children together, even as a hen gathereth her chickens under her wings, and ye would not!"

When Joseph's brothers fell down before him, Joseph said to them, "Fear not: for am I in the place of God?" (Gen. 50:19). Joseph assured them that he was not their judge because it was not his prerogative to judge.

Joseph then said to his brothers, "But as for you, ye thought evil against me; but God meant it unto good, to bring to pass, as it is this day, to save much people alive" (v. 20). Joseph realized that even though his brothers had had evil in mind when they sold him into slavery, "God planned it for good." Oh, that we might grasp the sovereignty of God as Joseph did. What a difference it makes when we see the hand of God even in adverse circumstances of life. Because Joseph had such a grasp of the sovereignty of God, there was no desire to retaliate. Instead, he told his brothers, "Therefore fear ye not: I will nourish you, and your little ones. And he comforted them, and spake kindly unto them" (v. 21).

As the biblical account concerning Joseph's life draws to a close, it says, "And Joseph dwelt in Egypt, he, and his father's house: and Joseph lived an hundred and ten years. And Joseph saw Ephraim's children of the third generation: the children also of Machir the son of Manasseh were brought up upon Joseph's knees" (vv. 22, 23). Joseph's 110 years amounted to a long and fruitful life. He was one of the Bible's greatest and sweetest characters who lived in simple trust in Jehovah. He was such a person because he was indwelt by God. The same God who lived in Joseph's life also lives in ours. Therefore, we, too, can live a life just as holy, separated and victorious as Joseph lived.

Crowning Example of Faith

The crowning example of Joseph's faith was expressed just before his death; therefore, it was also his final expression of faith. After all the years of prosperity for him and his people, his faith was as strong as ever. Joseph said to his brothers, "I die: and God will surely visit you, and bring you out of this land unto the land which he sware unto Abraham, to Isaac, and to Jacob" (v. 24). Joseph had an unswerving confidence in the fact that God would complete the program He had begun. The Scriptures then say, "And Joseph took an oath of the children of Israel, saying, God will visit you, and ye shall carry up my bones from hence" (v. 25).

Just as his father, Jacob, was determined that Egypt was not to be the final resting place for his bones, so was Joseph. Perhaps you ask, Did it really make that much difference where he was buried? It did to Joseph because God had made promises concerning the land that Jacob's descendants were to inherit. As these people served God, their hopes were fixed on that land and what God would do for them there. This was so important to Joseph that as he looked forward to the resurrection, he wanted to be resurrected from that special land that God had promised to them.

It was this final and crowning statement of faith which won Joseph his place in God's hall of fame; that is, chapter 11 of the Book of Hebrews. It was not Joseph's striking victory at Potiphar's house nor his vast administrative achievements that won him this place. Rather, it was this last commandment of faith concerning his bones. God's Word says that "by faith Joseph, when he died, made mention of the departing of the children of Israel; and gave commandment concerning his bones" (Heb. 11:22).

God is pleased when we trust Him and demonstrate our confidence in Him by the way we live. It is by this faith principle that God works in our lives. If we want to please the Lord more and glorify Him more, then we must start believing Him more and trusting Him more. When we really believe Him, we will act upon our faith because we have taken God at His word.

It is so easy for even Christians to have wrong concepts about what is really important. On that day when we stand before Christ to give an account of what we have done in the body for Him, there will be some amazing reversals of opinions about what is really important. Many things that we now consider so important will be insignificant when we stand before Him. We will discover that the most important thing was not how much we did in attempting to serve God but how much we believed God. True faith brings true action. The Judgment Seat of Christ is referred to in I Corinthians 3:13. Of this time it is said that "every man's work shall be made manifest: for the day shall declare it, because it shall be revealed by fire; and the fire shall try every man's work of what sort it is." The work will not be tried to see "how much" it is but to see "of what sort it is." In God's economy, quality is far more important than quantity.

As Joseph gave commandment concerning his body and made the children of Israel take an oath that they would do as he instructed, it may have been difficult for some of them to really believe that the nation would someday be led back to Canaan. In fact, many of them probably had no desire to return. After all, they were now prosperously settled in the richest sector of the land of Egypt. It would be difficult to think about giving up all of that and returning to the conditions they had experienced in Canaan. They might have reasoned, We are having such a wonderful time here, who wants to leave? Therefore, at a later time God had to allow severe testings and hardships to come on them to cause them to want to leave Egypt.

Joseph did not forget the promises that God had made to Abraham, Isaac and Jacob. He did not forget the purpose for which God had sent him to Egypt. Nor did he forget that the stay of Jacob's descendants in Egypt was not to be permanent. God had told Jacob, "I will go down with thee into Egypt; and I will also surely bring thee up again" (Gen. 46:4). Engraved on Joseph's heart was the heaven-born conviction that the stay of God's chosen family in Egypt was to be a temporary one.

In the World, Not of It

Although Joseph sojourned in a different land than Abraham, the same things were true of him as are said of Abraham in Hebrews 11:9,10: "By faith he [Abraham] sojourned in the land of promise, as in a strange country, dwelling in tabernacles with Isaac and Jacob, the heirs with him of the same promise: for he looked for a city which hath foundations, whose builder and maker is God." Although Abraham and Joseph lived in the world, they never became a part of the world—their eyes were fixed on that which is beyond.

It should also be true of present-day believers that even though we are in the world, we are not a part of the world. In His prayer before His crucifixion, the Lord Jesus Christ prayed for His own and said, "They are not of the world, even as I am not of the world" (John 17:16). Then He said, "As thou hast sent me into the world, even so have I also sent them into the world" (v. 18). These are very important verses for us to remember. We have been sent into this world as ambassadors for Christ, but we should never become part of the world's system. We are not to be isolated from the world, but we are to live insulated from the world.

When Pilate asked Jesus what He had done to be delivered by the chief priests, Jesus answered, "My kingdom is not of this world: if my kingdom were of this world, then would my servants fight, that I should not be delivered to the Jews: but now is my kingdom not from hence [from here]" (18:36). The Lord's kingdom is not of this world, and how wonderful it is to know that each Christian has been translated into His kingdom. Colossians 1:13 tells us that the Heavenly Father "hath delivered us from the power of darkness, and hath translated us into the kingdom of his dear Son." Hebrews 13:12-14 says, "Wherefore Jesus also, that he might sanctify the people with his own blood, suffered without the gate. Let us go forth therefore unto him without the camp, bearing his reproach. For here have we no continuing city, but we seek one to come." Abraham and Joseph realized this world was not their home; they were just passing through. Do you realize this?

The following song has been a blessing to me many times as I have thought about the believer's relationship to the world:

This World Is Not My Home
This world is not my home, I'm just a passing thru,
My treasures are laid up somewhere beyond the blue;
The angels beckon me from heaven's open door,
And I can't feel at home in this world anymore.

They're all expecting me, and that's one thing I know,
My Saviour pardoned me and now I onward go;
I know He'll take me thru tho I am weak and poor,
And I can't feel at home in this world anymore.

O Lord, you know I have no friend like you,
If heaven's not my home then Lord, what will I do?
The angels beckon me from heaven's open door,
And I can't feel at home in this world anymore.
                                        —Author Unknown

God had promised not only to Jacob but also to Abraham earlier that their descendants would eventually return from Egypt. In Genesis 15:13-16 God told Abraham that his descendants would serve another nation but that in the fourth generation they would return. Although in Joseph's time such a return might have seemed very remote, he had confidence in God that the promise would be kept. Joseph had peace about this because his attention was not on the materialism of the present but on God's program for the future. Might this also be true of us.

When a person's confidence is in God, he has perfect peace. Isaiah wrote: "Thou wilt keep him in perfect peace, whose mind is stayed on thee: because he trusteth in thee. Trust ye in the Lord for ever: for in the Lord Jehovah is everlasting strength" (26:3,4).

It is interesting to consider the results of the oath the children of Israel took that they would carry Joseph's bones to the land God had promised them. The Scriptures say that after the Passover when the children of Israel fled the land of Egypt, "God led the people about, through the way of the wilderness of the Red sea: and the children of Israel went up harnessed out of the land of Egypt. And Moses took the bones of Joseph with him: for he had straitly sworn the children of Israel, saying, God will surely visit you; and ye shall carry up my bones away hence with you" (Ex. 13:18,19). While Joseph was living, he had a mighty voice for God. After his death, his voice continued to speak. Think of the silent yet powerful testimony it was as the children of Israel carried Joseph's bones with them on the way to the Promised Land!

Joseph's Death

The oath having been made to carry up his bones to the land, the Scriptures say, "so Joseph died, being an hundred and ten years old: and they embalmed him, and he was put in a coffin in Egypt" (Gen. 50:26). It does not say that they put him in a grave; nor is it stated where the coffin was kept. But think of the reminder that this coffin containing Joseph's bones was to the children of Israel during those years. Even while they were comfortably living in Egypt, that coffin of bones was a constant reminder that someday they were to return to the land that God had promised them. It must have inspired their hearts with undying hope as they waited for that day of deliverance. Although Joseph's body had died, his faith and testimony had not died.

The coffin that contained Joseph's bones spoke of life as well as of death. It contained the remains of a person who had lived by faith in the promises of God. And because the coffin was to be carried to the land God had promised, it also spoke of resurrection.

After what may have been 200 years of watching and waiting, the coffin containing Joseph's bones was carried up out of Egypt. The children of Israel had it with them during their 40 years of wandering in the desert and probably about five more years in Canaan while they were conquering the land. Then, we are told in Joshua 24:32, "And the bones of Joseph, which the children of Israel brought up out of Egypt, buried they in Shechem, in a parcel of ground which Jacob bought of the sons of Hamor the father of Shechem for an hundred pieces of silver: and it became the inheritance of the children of Joseph." What a paradox it was that during their 40 years of faithlessness, the children of Israel carried that coffin of Joseph's bones which spoke of such great faith. The coffin was without burial or resting place. Neither did the Israelites have rest—there is no rest when faith is not put into action.

The Book of Exodus tells of the departure, or deliverance, of the Israelites from Egypt. In faith, Joseph spoke of this exodus which would be accomplished in God's time.

We believers living in the 20th century can also look forward to a glorious departure. The Apostle Paul wrote concerning the departure of the Church from this earth when he said, "Behold, I shew you a mystery; We shall not all sleep, but we shall all be changed, in a moment, in the twinkling of an eye, at the last trump: for the trumpet shall sound, and the dead shall be raised incorruptible, and we shall be changed" (I Cor. 15:51,52). This same comfort of hope is also referred to in I Thessalonians 4:13-18: "But I would not have you to be ignorant, brethren, concerning them which are asleep, that ye sorrow not, even as others which have no hope. For if we believe that Jesus died and rose again, even so them also which sleep in Jesus will God bring with him. For this we say unto you by the word of the Lord, that we which are alive and remain unto the coming of the Lord shall not prevent them which are asleep. For the Lord himself shall descend from heaven with a shout, with the voice of the archangel, and with the trump of God: and the dead in Christ shall rise first: then we which are alive and remain shall be caught up together with them in the clouds, to meet the Lord in the air: and so shall we ever be with the Lord. Wherefore comfort one another with these words." Do you know Jesus Christ as your Saviour? If so, these words concerning the Rapture of the Church from the earth will bring comfort to you, not fear.

The study of Joseph's life should cause us to realize the importance of being down to business with God as we live here on earth. Let us take seriously the words of Romans 13:11-14: "And that, knowing the time, that now it is high time to awake out of sleep: for now is our salvation nearer than when we believed. The night is far spent, the day is at hand: let us therefore cast off the works of darkness, and let us put on the armour of light. Let us walk honestly, as in the day; not in rioting and drunkenness, not in chambering and wantonness, not in strife and envying. But put ye on the Lord Jesus Christ, and make not provision for the flesh, to fulfil the lusts thereof."

Are you ready to meet Jesus Christ today? "Be ye therefore ready also: for the Son of man cometh at an hour when ye think not" (Luke 12:40). If you are not certain about your relationship with Jesus Christ, delay no longer. Make sure before it is eternally too late. Jesus Christ has promised, "He that heareth my word, and believeth on him that sent me, hath everlasting life, and shall not come into condemnation; but is passed from death unto life" (John 5:24).

When you are sure you are right with God, you will be able to look at life with a different perspective. You will then be able to look at the adverse conditions of this life and say, "God planned it for good."